Young Offenders: Children and crime in Ireland, 1850–1908

This book makes a valuable contribution to the existing literature on the history of state responses to young offenders through providing a comprehensive account of the early development of reformatory and industrial schools in Ireland.

Dr Clarissa Carden, Griffith University

This welcome study adds valuable insights into our understanding of the development of the Irish juvenile justice system. Curtin reveals insights into children's experiences of poverty and neglect, institutionalisation, and systems of punishment and reform, including convict transportation. This book not only adds to our understanding of juvenile justice in the nineteenth century but also illuminates the stories of post-Famine Ireland and the lives of some of its most vulnerable inhabitants.

Professor Heather Shore, Manchester Metropolitan University

… a new series from Cork University Press, Studies in Irish Crime History, … is doing a fantastic job of putting out entertaining, accessible and interesting titles.

Dr Lynsey Black, *Estudios Irlandeses Journal of Irish Studies*

Studies in Irish Crime History

Young Offenders: Children and crime in Ireland, 1850–1908

Geraldine Curtin

First published in 2025 by
Cork University Press
Boole Library
University College Cork
Cork T12 ND89
Ireland

Library of Congress Control Number: 2025942552

Distribution in the USA Longleaf Services, Chapel Hill, NC, USA.

© the author 2026

EU GPSR Authorised Representative: Sinéad Neville.
Email: corkuniversitypress@ucc.ie

All rights reserved. No part of this book may be reprinted or reproduced or utilised in any electronic, mechanical or other means, now known or hereafter invented, including photocopying and recording or otherwise, without either the prior written permission of the publisher or a licence permitting restricted copying in Ireland issued by the Irish Copyright Licensing Agency Ltd, 25 Denzille Lane, Dublin 2.

The right of Geraldine Curtin to be identified as the author of this Work has been asserted by her in accordance with the Copyright and Related Rights Acts 2000 to 2007.

British Library Cataloguing in Publication Data
A CIP catalogue record for this book is available in the British Library.

ISBN: 9781782050810

Printed by CPI in the UK

Design and typesetting by Alison Burns at Studio 10 Design, Cork

Cover image: Prisoner, Mountjoy Convict Prison, 1857.
Thomas A. Larcom photographs collection, Manuscripts and Archives Division, The New York Public Library.

www.corkuniversitypress.com

Contents

Acknowledgements	xi
List of Figures and Tables	xiii
Introduction	1
Chapter 1 **Criminal Children after the Famine**	7
Chapter 2 **The First Reformatories**	37
Chapter 3 **'Unstained by Criminality'? Poor and criminal children, 1868–80**	79
Chapter 4 **Saving Children From 'Moral Ruin': 1880–1908**	127
Conclusion	157
Notes	163
Bibliography	190
Index	204

Studies in Irish Crime History

SERIES EDITORS: Richard Mc Mahon and Ciara Molloy

This book series explores how crime history can offer new ways of understanding Irish society. It maps and critically engages with the actions and beliefs of those who often held a marginal position in Irish society, their relationship to the broader population and, crucially, their interactions with those in positions of authority. The history of the murderer, the prostitute, the thief, the bank robber, the vagrant, the white-collar criminal, among others, and their relationship to the police officer, the lawyer, the jury, the judge and the hangman will be explored to arrive at a deeper sense of the conflicts and contradictions that underpinned Irish life and continue to shape it into the present. The series also aims to explore the construction and meaning of key concepts such as 'crime' and 'evil' and the impact of such concepts on the individual, society and the state. In doing so, the series will embrace but also cut across key aspects of political, legal, economic, social and cultural history and raise questions about the nature of Irish society over time in fruitful and novel ways.

1. Brian Hanley, *Republicanism, Crime and Paramilitary Policing in Ireland, 1916–2020*.

2. Aogán Mulcahy, *Crime and Conflict in Northern Ireland, 1920–2022*.

3. Brian Griffin, *Crime and the Criminal Classes in Ireland, 1870–1920*.

4. Geraldine Curtin, *Young Offenders: Children and crime in Ireland, 1850–1908*.

Acknowledgements

I am indebted to many people who have helped me in the preparation of this book. It began life as a PhD thesis. Dr Caitriona Clear was my supervisor and her integrity, wisdom and support made it possible. I am grateful to the series editors, Dr Richard Mc Mahon and Dr Ciara Molloy, for their meticulous editorial work and for their advice, and to the people at Cork University Press for all the help they have given me.

I had the very good fortune on my first visit to the National Archives in Dublin many years ago to meet with Gregory O'Connor. His depth of knowledge and his kindness were greatly appreciated and I still miss him when I visit the archives. Brian Donnelly, and Peter and Carl, in the Reading Room, have been of great assistance, especially when I was looking for obscure references. I am thankful to Deirdre O'Connor, SSL, in the Archives of the Sisters of St Louis for her hospitality. Noelle Dowling in the Archdiocese of Dublin Archives provided me with invaluable sources.

I would like to acknowledge the New York Public Library, and their Permissions and Reproduction Services, for their generosity in making available the extraordinary photographs of prisoners taken in Mountjoy in 1857. When I first contacted John Kearney of the Offaly Historical & Archaeological Society for permission to use images taken in the Philipstown reformatory he was most generous and accommodating. Offaly Archives have been equally helpful in sharing their resources with me. The reprographics service of the National Archives in Dublin provided images from their collections and I am grateful to them.

Countless colleagues, friends and family provided practical and moral support when I needed advice, help or just good company. At the James Hardiman Library, Eimhin, Deirdre, Rioghna, Gabi and Catriona each helped in different ways, and my former colleague Mary came to my aid when tiredness clouded my judgement. Thank you to Tom Kenny for the gentle encouragement and to Michael and my wonderful neighbours for the support, laughter and distraction.

Photo Credits:

Thomas A. Larcom photographs collection, Manuscripts and Archives Division, The New York Public Library

National Archives, PRIS/1/21/02, Galway Gaol Register

Offaly History Collection, Offaly Archives

National Archives, GPB/PEN/1885/85, William McAvina, number 10560

National Archives, CRF/1871/F/14, letter from Mary Fleming to her parents

List of Figures and Tables

FIGURES

Figure 1	'Some of the more serious offenders … in Mountjoy', 1857	6
Figure 2	Galway gaol register	10
Figure 3	Tailor shop, Philipstown reformatory	94
Figure 4	William McAvina at the beginning and end of his prison sentence	103
Figure 5	Letter from Mary Fleming, Spark's Lake reformatory	106

TABLES

Table 1	Inmates in reformatories, 1869	51
Table 2	Committals to prison, 1854 to 1870	76
Table 3	Categories of child prisoners, 1854 and 1869	116

Introduction

In the summer of 1857 a photographer was sent to Mountjoy convict prison in Dublin to capture images of prisoners. The pictures of sixty-four inmates were subsequently bound in an album that described them as '[s]ome of the more serious offenders' incarcerated there.[1] Most are unnamed, and while no details are given about the prisoners or the nature of their crimes, it is obvious that some are young children. Mountjoy had opened seven years earlier as part of a complex and innovative system that aimed to reform its inmates. Robert Netterville, the governor of the prison, wrote that several of his young prisoners appeared to have 'relinquished their vicious propensities'. The head schoolmaster reported that most of the eighty-three boys taught by him were able to read 'standard works of literature with ease and intelligence'.[2] Despite this apparent success, however, changing attitudes to child criminals in the middle of the nineteenth century meant that a new approach to their treatment was being considered.[3] Government enquiries and the work of reformers in Britain and Ireland from the middle of the nineteenth century gave rise to new institutions and separate treatment for children who were convicted of crime.

Poor and criminal children in Ireland in the nineteenth century have been the subject of a number of studies. Joseph Robins' *The Lost Children* is a wide-ranging study of 'abandoned infant ... destitute orphan and other deprived children' in Ireland from 1700 to 1900.[4]

Industrial schools, from their foundation to 1908, are the focus of Jane Barnes' *Irish Industrial Schools*.[5] From the 1990s, studies began to emerge that increasingly questioned the supposedly positive impact of institutions for the care of children on their lives and the lives of their families, and instead posited them as mechanisms for the 'regulation of the poor'.[6] This questioning coincided with the publication of the testimonies of those who had been inside the institutions, particularly the industrial schools, in the twentieth century. Mary Raftery and Eoin O'Sullivan's *Suffer the Little Children*[7] in 1999 and the Ryan Report[8] a decade later exposed widespread abuse of children in industrial schools and reformatories. As the voices of children emerged in these studies and in official enquiries we began to learn that 'human testimony, when placed alongside the official record, is at its most powerful'.[9]

Another type of institution for older offenders, the borstal, was examined by Nial Osborough and Conor Reidy.[10] Ian Miller has argued that reformatories and industrial schools were 'initially designed as healthy environments' that contrasted with what were considered to be the morally and physically unhealthy backgrounds of the children.[11] Paul Sargent explored the system of juvenile justice from a governmentality perspective from the mid-nineteenth to the early twenty-first century.[12] More recently, scholars outside of Ireland have begun to shift their focus away from reforms and legislative changes and towards the life courses and stories of poor and marginalised children,[13] and to the victims of crime.[14]

This book begins as the Great Famine of the 1840s was coming to an end.[15] While previous studies have looked at legislative reforms and institutional change, this study has made extensive use of both 'official' and 'unofficial' sources to try to create a picture of the lives of children who came to the attention of the justice system in Ireland, and to look closely at how this system evolved in Ireland over six decades. There were many official enquiries into poor and criminal children in the period covered by this book, and these official reports, as well as those of the inspectors and reformers who visited the institutions, are valuable sources which help to create a picture of how children were regarded and treated at this time. Official sources, however, while useful and extensive, have many limitations. As will be seen in the reformatory inspectors' reports, the officials who wrote them were often concerned with presenting the institutions they visited in a positive light, and their reports were consequently skewed. The children themselves are almost completely silent in the official records and historical discourse. They did not leave memoirs behind to tell us what they experienced or how they felt. What is left to us are the fragments of their life stories that appear in the records. On rare occasions, in newspapers and in letters that survive, we hear hints of their voices and those of their families. Newspaper reports of trials are used in this study to allow us to witness the sometimes defiant, often frightened and occasionally humorous behaviour of children and their families in court. Accounts of those who were incarcerated in, or who visited, the institutions where children were held also give us a glimpse of conditions within their walls, and this is the first study to look in detail at the reformatories that were established after 1858. Prison registers are closely examined to create a picture of the nature and extent of reported child criminality, and photographs of those who were incarcerated allow us to see the faces of children too often characterised by statistics and official rhetoric.

The poverty and social disturbance caused by the Great Famine gave rise to a dramatic increase in crime in Ireland in the mid-nineteenth century. Chapter 1 looks at its impact on the lives of children. Thousands were sent to gaol or transported to penal colonies. Thousands more found themselves in workhouses, and others 'wandered abroad', begging or stealing to survive. While Ireland was still emerging from the effects of the Famine, reformers in other countries were proposing alternatives to imprisonment for children. A small but influential group of Irish people began to look at reformatories that had been established in Britain, France and Belgium, and to propose that similar institutions be opened in Ireland. Chapter 2 examines the institutions that opened after the passing of the Reformatory Schools (Ireland) Act of 1858, with a particular focus on religion, funding, discipline and daily life within the institutions. The chapter ends with an appraisal of the outcomes of, and the challenges experienced by, these first reformatories whose founding principles shaped a system of institutional care of children that would survive in Ireland well into the twentieth century.

Once reformatories had been established for criminal

juveniles, reformers focused with renewed interest on Ireland's poor children. In 1868 legislation was passed to facilitate the opening of industrial schools. As was the case with reformatories, children would be sent to the new schools by the courts, and the funding and management structures of these institutions were also similar. Provision was made in the new law for very young criminal children to be sent to industrial schools instead of reformatories. Yet, while there were now two new types of residential school for the incarceration of criminal children, most were still sent to gaol to serve out their sentences. Chapter 3 examines the three types of institution and considers how children were treated in each of them. It also looks at the crimes for which children were convicted, and at the behaviour of children and their families in court. By the late nineteenth century, there was increasing pressure to remove children from the adult criminal justice system, and the final chapter looks at how societal and legislative changes helped to bring this about. The report of a government commission that investigated Irish reformatory and industrial schools in the 1880s is examined and it will be shown that, in many ways, the enquiry failed the children who had been and would be sent to reformatories.

This book looks in detail at the treatment of child criminals in Ireland from 1850, when the Great Famine was coming to an end, to the passing of the Children Act in 1908. Woven into the narrative are the stories of the children, women and men who shaped and were the subjects of the juvenile justice system in Ireland in the late nineteenth and early twentieth centuries.

Figure 1: 'Some of the more serious offenders … in Mountjoy', 1857

Chapter 1

Criminal Children after the Famine

'Shoals of vagrants'

MARTIN CORMACK appeared before a court in County Galway in April 1850 charged with the crime of 'malicious trespass on [a] potato field'. He was found guilty and sentenced to three weeks' imprisonment in Galway gaol[1] and 'to be twice whipped'.[2] A month earlier, an Armagh court found Margaret Wallace guilty of burglary and sentenced her to ten years' transportation. On 9 January 1851, she was put aboard the convict ship *Black Friar*, bound for Australia.[3] Martin was eleven years old and Margaret was thirteen. Both served their sentences in the company of prisoners of all ages whose crimes varied from petty theft to murder and manslaughter.

Martin and Margaret had been incarcerated in a prison system that was in crisis. The Great Irish Famine of the 1840s had resulted in the deaths of more than one million people. Many others who survived lived in a state of hunger and homelessness. In May 1851, a quarter of a million people were in Irish workhouses, out of a total population of six-and-a-half million.[4] More than 100,000 workhouse inmates were children.[5] The Vagrancy Act of 1847 provided for magistrates to commit beggars to gaol.[6] By the middle of the nineteenth century the prison network comprised three layers that reached into every community in Ireland. There were 112 bridewells, or lock-ups, which were situated in towns where petty sessions courts were held. Over forty local gaols held prisoners for sentences usually ranging from twenty-four hours to two years. In 1850 a carceral building boom culminated in the completion of Mountjoy, Ireland's 'model prison', built to hold 496 prisoners in separate cells.[7] These prisoners were convicts, initially destined for transportation but later held for longer sentences as part of a system devised by the directors of convict prisons, led by Walter Crofton.[8] Children could be found in each of these layers. At this time criminal children over the age of seven could be treated in the same way as adults.[9]

Any perceived progress that was being made in the prison system in the mid-nineteenth century was brought to a sudden and tumultuous stop by external forces. Prison inspectors wrote of the effect that the 'terrible catastrophe' of the Famine had on the gaols: 'industrial works given up ... separation unattempted, and disease and death increasing'.[10] The Vagrancy Act brought thousands of destitute prisoners into the system. Children as young as two years of age began to appear in gaols. The prison registers recorded their crimes as 'asking alms'.[11] In 1853 there were 5,239 committals to prison of children aged sixteen and under for the crime of vagrancy.[12] Many destitute people deliberately committed acts of petty vandalism so that they could gain access to the food and shelter of the gaols. Even those already in institutions sometimes saw gaol as a better alternative. A great number of young boys under twelve years of age, the inspectors noted, 'committed offences in the workhouses for the purpose of being transferred to the prisons, wherein the dietary is better'.[13]

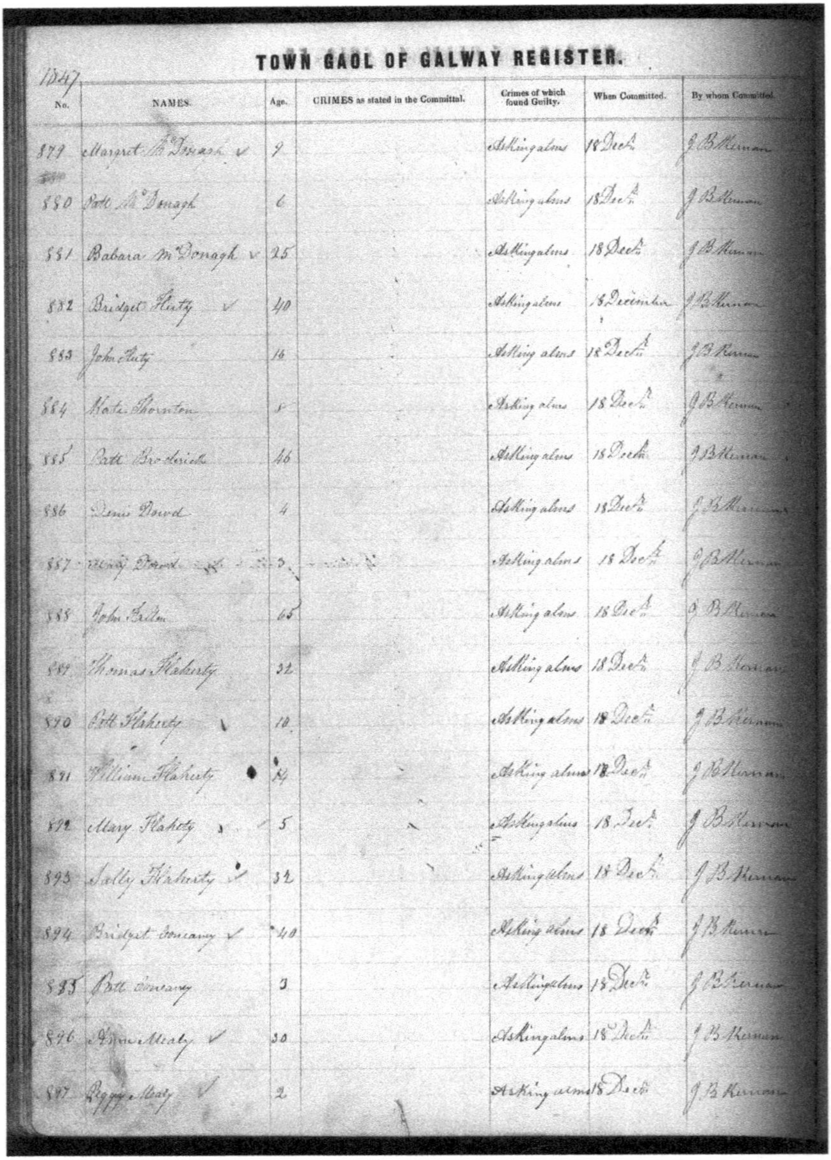

TOWN GAOL OF GALWAY REGISTER.

1847

No.	NAMES.	Age.	CRIMES as stated in the Committal.	Crimes of which found Guilty.	When Committed.	By whom Committed.
879	Margret McDonagh	9		Asking alms	18 Decr	J B Kernan
880	Patt McDonagh	6		Asking alms	18 Decr	J B Kernan
881	Babara McDonagh	25		Asking alms	18 Decr	J B Kernan
882	Bridget Heaty	40		Asking alms	18 December	J B Kernan
883	John Heaty	16		Asking alms	18 Decr	J B Kernan
884	Kate Thornton	8		Asking alms	18 Decr	J B Kernan
885	Patt Broderick	46		Asking alms	18 Decr	J B Kernan
886	Denis Dowd	4		Asking alms	18 Decr	J B Kernan
887	Mary Dowd	3		Asking alms	18 Decr	J B Kernan
888	John Fallon	65		Asking alms	18 Decr	J B Kernan
889	Thomas Flaherty	32		Asking alms	18 Decr	J B Kernan
890	Patt Flaherty	10		Asking alms	18 Decr	J B Kernan
891	William Flaherty	14		Asking alms	18 Decr	J B Kernan
892	Mary Flaherty	5		Asking alms	18 Decr	J B Kernan
893	Sally Flaherty	32		Asking alms	18 Decr	J B Kernan
894	Bridget Donneany	40		Asking alms	18 Decr	J B Kernan
895	Patt Donneany	3		Asking alms	18 Decr	J B Kernan
896	Anne Mealy	30		Asking alms	18 Decr	J B Kernan
897	Peggy Mealy	2		Asking alms	18 Decr	J B Kernan

Figure 2: Galway gaol register

Outside of the state institutions – the gaols and workhouses – the very poor were doing what they could to survive. Displaced and hungry rural people sought relief in the towns. In their report of 1850, the prison inspectors noted that 'shoals of vagrants' wandered the country.[14] Martin Cormack and his family were part of this group. Following his arrest for trespassing on a potato field in 1850, members of his family, in groups or separately, were arrested. In June his father and three siblings were brought to court for begging at Athenry. He and four of his younger siblings were arrested for vagrancy in January 1851 and sent to gaol for twenty-two days. Further arrests of different Cormack [Cormick] family groupings followed in that year for crimes including threatening to break windows – frequently associated with attempts by the destitute to gain shelter in gaol – while his mother Catherine was imprisoned in May for deserting her children, probably by leaving them in the workhouse. In 1852 she was sent to gaol for vagrancy along with her two older children. After this, Martin disappears from the records.[15]

The prison inspectors described how '[t]his wandering population has been turned to account by professional thieves and divided into gangs' who 'prowl[ed]' about looking for opportunities to steal. They estimated that a quarter of all petty larceny in Dublin was committed by children, either the 'destitute and friendless orphans of those who fell victims to the famine' or the children of 'dissolute parents, who have been educated in crime'.[16] One official of the Poor Law system conceded that in many cases it was destitution, or 'actual want', that caused children to commit crime.[17] The inspectors of prisons agreed that hunger drove many people to crime who did not normally 'fall below the level of average morality'. Gangs of people, they wrote, were 'setting' houses for opportunities to steal.[18]

Ireland's gaols were filled beyond capacity. In 1850 Galway county gaol, which had accommodation for 110 prisoners, held a daily average of 384. Ennis gaol held four times the number of prisoners for which it was built.[19] The Dublin Metropolitan Police arrested 16,557 children aged fifteen and under.[20] In many gaols, young and old, diseased and healthy, beggars and serious offenders were crowded into small cells. The prison authorities reduced the food allowed to prisoners. Children under ten years of age were allowed 5 ounces of meal and a half-pint of milk for breakfast, 10 ounces of bread and a half-pint of milk for lunch, and 4 ounces of bread and a naggin and a half of milk for supper. As well as deterring those who sought shelter in the gaols, it was hoped that the cost of running a prison system that was in crisis might be reduced. The prison inspectors expressed their unhappiness with the Vagrancy Act because of the thousands of naked, diseased and 'miserable' human beings it brought into the system.[21]

Richmond bridewell, the gaol for Dublin city males, was where most child prisoners were sent. In 1851, there were 390 committals of children aged ten and under, and 2,512 of those aged eleven to fifteen were sent to Richmond.[22] The governor wrote that:

In one day last month 145 Prisoners were committed, of which 103 were vagrants, and, on the following day, we discharged 154, the most of them being well known to have come here every day for their dinner and lodging for the night. Their conduct on passing out was disgraceful beyond conception, and they had become such a terror and nuisance to the neighbourhood that an escort of mounted Police had to wait on the road every morning to disperse and pursue them.[23]

Many of these wandering inmates brought contagious diseases with them. The governor's solution was to strip the vagrants, shave their hair, and have them scrubbed from head to foot by other inmates. The able-bodied worked the treadmill, while the old, infirm and children were put to work stone-breaking. Those who did not perform their work adequately had half their dinner withheld. This, he believed, would deter them from using his gaol as a refuge.[24]

Within the prison system, there were structures to help young prisoners. Many gaols had schools. When James W. Kavanagh, head inspector of the Commissioners of Education, visited prison schools in the early 1850s, he found that nine had submitted themselves for inspection by the National Board of Education.[25] Richmond was one of these. The schoolmaster, Mr Hamill, was praised by the prison inspectors for doing a good job in difficult circumstances. He told them that a system that fostered the reformation of children would be preferable to the harsh punishments which the governor was adopting in order to reduce recommittals of young boys. He taught them 'reading, writing, arithmetic and some of the rudiments of grammar and geography' and it was reported that some made 'considerable advancement'.[26]

The task of educating poor, criminal children in gaol was challenging. When John Mitchel was being held in Spike Island convict prison awaiting transportation in 1848, he met 'a tall, gentleman-like person, in black but rather over-worn clothes'. The man was Edward Walsh, 'author of *Mo craoibhin cno*, and other sweet songs'. With tears in his eyes, Walsh told him that 'he had accepted the office of teacher to a school they keep here for small convicts – a very wretched office, indeed ...'.[27] Many gaols had skilled turnkeys who could teach trades. In Clonmel the prison inspectors noted that they appeared to be 'intelligent' men who taught the prisoners shoemaking, tailoring, weaving, carpentry and smithwork. Some prisoners, they were told, left gaol as trained workers who were less likely to re-offend.[28] The head schoolmaster in Mountjoy, while admitting that prisoners looked forward to attending school because it broke the 'tedious monotony of the separate cell', held lofty ideals about the power of education to change their lives. Every new prisoner was brought to the schoolroom and assessed, after which he was given books 'suited to his capacity and attainments', which he could keep in his cell. The juveniles made considerable progress in literary education, and many progressed to the intermediate prison in Smithfield, where they had greater freedom and more privileges.[29]

Despite these efforts at improvement, there was growing concern, both internationally and in Ireland, that child prisoners should not be incarcerated with adult offenders. This concern was for the welfare of the children themselves and for society, which, it was felt, would suffer the consequences of the 'contamination' of the young prisoners by older offenders. The Catholic chaplain in Spike Island believed that the children held there were damaged, mentally and physically, by confinement and strict discipline, and called for more opportunities for 'exercise and hilarity'.[30] In 1857 a sum of £10,000 was set aside for the building of a penal reformatory at Lusk in County Dublin where young prisoners undergoing longer sentences could be imprisoned separately from adults.[31] This institution would never be built, however, as the debates around criminal children brought penal reform in a new direction.

'Reformation with due correction'

Margaret Wallace was one of the last Irish children to be transported.[32] The 'moral sewer' which many people now considered transportation to be had grown increasingly unpopular, both in the countries from which convicts were transported and in those to which they were sent.[33] In 1847 a House of Lords committee was convened to investigate the two most pressing issues in criminal law: juvenile offenders and transportation.[34] It took evidence from prison governors, chaplains, inspectors and judges. John D'Arcy, the governor of Ennis gaol, told the committee that he kept his child prisoners separate from adult offenders and allowed them 'judicious treatment' with the assistance of his schoolmaster and chaplain. Some of these young prisoners, he said, left his gaol sufficiently trained in a trade to be 'capable of earning their Bread'. He believed that a 'moderate flogging' of between twelve and twenty lashes with a birch rod, 'in the same way that Boys are punished at School', should be substituted for imprisonment for some juvenile offenders.[35]

The committee sought the opinions of twelve Irish judges. The lord chief justice deferred to the opinion of Dr Harty, the medical officer for the Dublin gaols. He told the committee that the case of juvenile offenders in Dublin was 'truly pitiable' because they were often orphaned or deserted children, or children who 'were driven by their very Parents to seek Support in thieving'.[36] With regard to the treatment of young criminals, many of the judges agreed with the manner in which Baron Pennefather, an 'able, conscientious judge'[37] with five decades' experience, dealt with them. He made enquiries about the circumstances of the child after conviction, and if he believed that they were not a hardened offender, would sentence them to imprisonment with hard labour, 'suited to the Age or Sex', or release them to the care of their friends or relations if they could guarantee their good behaviour. In the case of hardened offenders, he sentenced them to transportation.[38]

In their recommendations, the committee concluded that 'the contamination of a Gaol as Gaols are usually managed may often prove fatal, and must always be hurtful to Boys committed for a first offence'. These boys, they believed, were 'trained to the worst of Crimes' while in gaol. They recommended that children being tried for minor offences could be dealt with summarily by the lower courts and sentenced to either a short imprisonment or a whipping. In order to prevent re-offending, they concluded that the system of prison discipline should be improved to include the 'Benefits of good Training and of sound moral and religious Instruction'. While they agreed with their witnesses that transportation should be retained for the most serious offenders, the challenge now became 'the Reformation and ... Restoration to Society' of prisoners, especially the very young, who would in the future be incarcerated at home.[39]

Two months after the committee presented their report to parliament, new legislation was passed 'for the more speedy trial and punishment of juvenile offenders' in England and Wales.[40] A year later, a similar act was passed for Ireland.[41] It provided for children judged to be aged fourteen and under,[42] charged with the crime of simple larceny or similar crimes, to be tried in the lower courts and therefore avoid being held in gaol awaiting trial. The maximum punishments allowed by these courts for juveniles were three months' imprisonment, a fine not exceeding £3, or to be 'privately whipped'. The governor of Ennis gaol had objected to boys being whipped 'through the Town';[43] this new law ended such practices. If parents or friends of the child objected to such a trial and preferred to have the case heard before a jury, they could choose to do so. The new law recognised that children were a separate group within the criminal justice system requiring different treatment, but for some it did not go far enough.

Mary Carpenter was the daughter of a Unitarian minister and had established a ragged school for the education of very poor children in Bristol in 1846.[44] She worked in the school with children who had been imprisoned, and she became vehemently opposed to imprisonment as a way of dealing with most juvenile criminals. Disappointed with the outcome of the 1847 committee, she began to correspond with prison chaplains and judges, and in particular with Matthew Davenport Hill, the recorder of Birmingham. In 1851 she published a book advocating the setting up of reformatory schools for criminal children, a system which had been established in Europe.[45] Described as a 'brilliant, volatile, passionate and arrogant woman', Carpenter's work would 'dominate the history of the management of juvenile delinquency' for decades to come.[46] She organised a conference in Birmingham in 1851 which generated enough political pressure to bring about another government enquiry, this time solely devoted to the problem of how to deal with young criminals.

The committee set out to 'inquire into the present Treatment of Criminal and Destitute Juveniles', and to investigate how the penal system might be changed to provide such children with industrial training that combined 'Reformation with due Correction'. It sat from May to June 1852 and examined twenty-three witnesses. Mary Carpenter gave evidence of her experience in the ragged school (a term she disliked, preferring free day school), and of how boys who returned after serving a prison sentence were 'hardened'. 'The present system', she said, 'renders every boy who is imprisoned far more dangerous to society afterwards'. She told the committee that she had visited two institutions for criminal children in Britain – Stretton-on-Dunsmore and Redhill – and had studied the two great European reformatories, the Rauhe Haus in Hamburg and Mettray in France. When asked for her opinion on the treatment of criminal children, she said that she would first remove the child from his 'evil associates', then 'enlist the will of the child in the work' and 'act upon his spiritual nature'. In her proposed reformatories, children would be treated with kindness and religious and moral education would form a key component of their training. The schools should, she believed, be partly funded by the state.[47]

The only Irish witness who travelled to London at the behest of the committee was John Ball, a Poor Law commissioner. Before coming to London, he had sent a circular to the inspectors of all the workhouses in Ireland, asking them to provide information on the numbers of children who had been released from gaol and subsequently sought admission to the workhouses. Their replies, which he submitted to the committee, give an account of the fractured lives of children who moved between the two pillars of welfare and punishment in mid nineteenth-century Ireland – the workhouse and the gaol. While some of the inspectors told Ball that such children were very few in their districts, in some areas, such as Galway, the governor of the gaol referred discharged children to the relieving officer of the Poor Law union so that they might gain admittance to the workhouse. In almost all cases the guardians of the workhouses refused to admit them. The inspector for Galway and Mayo wrote that such children brought a 'spirit of insubordination and turbulence' into the workhouse. It was claimed that child paupers who had been in gaol convinced some of the younger boys to leave the workhouse to lead lives of 'idleness and vice'. In Cork a head constable told of young thieves who 'rob, bury in the ground the proceeds of their plunder, and enter the workhouse ... until the heat of pursuit after them has abated'. There had, he said, been complaints from the victims of boys who had escaped the workhouse to commit robberies. Such problems were most prevalent in large towns and cities, where, like the freed prisoners in Dublin, discharged workhouse paupers congregated and were more visible. However, John Ball told the committee that there existed in Ireland only a small class of criminal children who 'oscillated' between the gaols and workhouses, mostly boys, and that there were very few girls that he considered to be 'permanently criminal and destitute'. He endorsed the view that juvenile offenders should be held in separate institutions, supported by the state, and managed or overseen by charitable or religious bodies.[48]

When the investigation reconvened after the prorogation of parliament, John Ball was brought on to the committee. In April 1853 they took evidence from three Irish witnesses: James Corry Connellan, the inspector of prisons; Edward Senior, a Poor Law commissioner;

and Walter Berwick, a Cork judge. The most compelling evidence came from Berwick. He told the committee that he had tried 11,560 people since December 1847, and estimated that one-third of them were children. He told them of a young girl who had been brought before the courts for the crime of '[m]alicious injury to a turnip field'. She was a pauper who had eaten a raw turnip from the workhouse garden. She was sent to Cork gaol, 100 miles from Castletown workhouse where she had been living, to serve a sentence of one month with hard labour. She appeared in court again shortly after her discharge from gaol for the crimes of begging and glass-breaking. She told the court that she had no money for food or lodging and had broken the glass so that she might get food and shelter in gaol. Berwick made inquiries after her discharge and found that she had become a 'bad character'. He believed that sending children to gaol for begging criminalised them. He told the committee that he frequently tried children who were so small that he had to ask the turnkey to hold them up in the dock so that he could see them. The proper place for such children, he believed, was the workhouse.[49]

All three of the Irish witnesses supported the establishment of separate institutions for the incarceration of juvenile offenders in Ireland. James Corry Connellan had visited reformatories in France and England, and, while he believed that there 'was not at all the same amount of debauchery' in the juvenile criminal population of Ireland compared to London, he thought that Ireland would benefit from such institutions. He suggested beginning with an experiment – twin institutions, side by side, one penal and one reformatory. The former, operating on a more punitive principle, would act as a warning to the residents of the reformatory, which in turn would be an inducement for the children in the penal school to behave well so that they might be sent to the less strict discipline of the reformatory.[50] While Edward Senior also supported separate establishments for criminal children, he identified a difficulty which they might present in Ireland because of the poverty of the people: 'If you establish a perfectly healthy, happy-looking school, with well-fed children, doing light agricultural work ... such an asylum [would be] an object of hope rather than of fear'. Senior's solution to this problem was to make the schools as unattractive as possible, with a diet that was sufficient to keep the children healthy and no more. While many of the English and French reformers believed that small numbers of children, based on a 'family system', was best, he disagreed with them and proposed large institutions with up to 500 children. Senior also disagreed with Walter Berwick with regard to the incarceration of children for vagrancy. He supported the existing vagrancy laws, provided they were 'humanely and wisely carried out'. However, Senior believed that children who were frequently convicted for vagrancy should be sent to reformatories. He concurred with John Ball that Irish children shared a particular characteristic – 'the element of hope is very active in their minds'. For the future reformatory children of Ireland, he thought that the best incentive for them would be free passage to America at the expiration of their sentences.[51]

The committee recommended the opening of reformatory schools so that criminal children might be 'converted into virtuous, honest and industrious citizens'.[52] In Britain there was a strong tradition of voluntary effort in intervention with criminal children. The Philanthropic Society had been established in London in 1788 and had opened houses for training juvenile criminals.[53] A group of Warwickshire magistrates had founded a reformatory school for children in Stretton-on-Dunsmore in 1818 and a number of landowners had given land and money for others throughout England.[54] Many of the British reformatories were modelled on the penal agricultural colony for children at Mettray in France. Established in 1840 by a judge, Frédéric-Auguste Demetz, the colony was based on the 'family system', whereby the children lived in houses that were intended to replicate family homes and were supervised by specially trained staff.[55] In Bristol Mary Carpenter had opened a reformatory for boys in 1852 and one for girls in 1854. Government intervention came with the establishment of Parkhurst prison for the exclusive incarceration of boys in 1838. Mary Carpenter was highly critical of Parkhurst, and she and others continued to lobby for government support for reformatories. In 1854 they were successful, and the Act for the Better Care and Reformation of Youthful Offenders in Great Britain was passed.[56] The act made it permissible for courts to give children under sixteen years of age a sentence of two to five years in a reformatory in addition to a prison sentence. It also gave power to the Treasury to support the maintenance of children in such reformatories which would be established and managed by voluntary groups. The last line of the new legislation stated that '[t]his Act shall not apply to Ireland'.

Establishment of the reformatory system

In January 1854 an article appeared in the *Irish Quarterly Review* entitled 'Our Juvenile Criminals: The school-master or the gaoler'. The author wrote that '[t]he great majority of our prisons are but the seminaries of vice'. Parental example and 'parental precept' were 'sure sources of crime', according to the article, with children being sent out by parents to beg, steal and engage in prostitution, 'and if they return to their wretched homes – their kennels – unprovided with the required sum, blows and starvation are the unfailing penalties'. The author quoted Mary Carpenter, who wrote that an 'undisciplined childhood' without 'moral or religious influence' was the cause of juvenile crime.[57]

First published in 1851, the *Review* began its life as a periodical for members of the Irish bar. Its first issues contained articles relating to legal matters, literature, art and cultural history. By 1853, however, the emphasis of some of its articles had shifted to 'the education of the poor of the Kingdoms, and the training of young criminals into righteous and honest men',[58] and this theme supplanted most other legal matters until 1857. Since the authors wrote anonymously, it is difficult to know whether this editorial shift was due to a change in personnel. It is known that, for at least a substantial part of its ten-year existence, the editors of the *Review* were

Patrick Joseph Murray and J.T. Gilbert,[59] and Murray's later work would strongly indicate that he was responsible for the many articles and hundreds of pages which the *Review* dedicated to the subject of ragged, reformatory and industrial schools. By 1854 the *Review* included a '[q]uarterly record of the progress of reformatory and ragged schools, and of the improvement of prison discipline'. Much of the material in the early articles was based on the work of Mary Carpenter, Matthew Davenport Hill and English clerics and prison chaplains such as Sydney Turner, John Clay, Joseph Kingsmill and John Field. In 1856 Murray wrote that he had 'worked, anxiously, with thought, pen, and tongue, for five years' to support the reformatory movement in Ireland.[60]

In February 1856 the Irish chief secretary, Edward Horsman, brought a '[b]ill for the better care and reformation of juvenile offenders in Ireland' before the House of Commons.[61] The bill was similar to the British legislation and was met with vehement opposition in the house. Vincent Scully, MP for Cork, said that it gave 'too great facilities to the county magistrates to proselytise the children who might be sent to the juvenile reformatories'. The member for Dungarvan, John Maguire, was more direct and much more colourful in his opinion of the proposed legislation:

> In Ireland there was a great rage for proselytism, and religion and charity very often masqueraded themselves in that country in a very strange garb. He knew several people, kind and good, and others perhaps not

so, who made great sacrifices for the purpose of extending ragged schools. They could not break down the faith of higher and better fed people, so they picked up the very scrapings of the streets, and added them to the list of members of the Established Church.[62]

The 'rage for proselytism' to which Maguire referred was to become a crucial factor in shaping the Irish reformatory legislation and the way in which the reformatory system evolved. Protestant missions to Ireland had seen the opportunity for large-scale conversion of poor Irish Catholics. The most active proselytising group in Ireland in the middle of the nineteenth century was the Society for Irish Church Missions (hereafter ICM). By mid-century, the mission had opened twenty-one churches, forty-nine schools and four orphanages. Most of these were in the poorest areas of Dublin and Connemara.[63] Children became the focus of the attention of the missionaries.

The Catholic hierarchy was actively opposed to all attempts to bring Irish children under the influence of the Protestant faith. In the west of Ireland, John MacHale, the Catholic archbishop of the large diocese of Tuam, had opposed the opening of national schools in his diocese because he believed they were being used to convert Catholic children.[64] Protestant missions filled the vacuum in many places and provided free education to the children of the poor. On the streets of Dublin and in the byways of Connemara, Protestant and Catholic activists engaged at times in physical tussles for poor children. One such Catholic activist, Maria Murray, went from school to school in Dublin snatching children from the Protestant proselytisers. Her advice to the archbishop of Dublin, Paul Cullen, was to open a Catholic school for such children.[65]

The Catholic Church escalated its offensive against the ICM from the 1850s and began to defend its position and strengthen its influence. In 1851 at a meeting in the Rotunda in Dublin a large group of prominent Catholics, chaired by Cullen, endorsed the formation of an independent party in parliament and launched the Catholic Defence Association. John Maguire attended the meeting.[66] He became one of a group of Irish MPs in Westminster that came to be known as the 'Pope's Brass Band'. This group was strongly opposed to Horsman's bill. Between February and June of 1856 these MPs and leading Catholics in Britain were in correspondence with Paul Cullen. Vincent Scully replied to a letter from the archbishop on 21 February that he would 'do all that may now remain in my humble power' regarding the bill. On the same date, Thomas Meagher, MP for Waterford, wrote to Cullen that a meeting of members who were opposed to the bill had been held and a committee formed. They had secured a postponement of the legislation.[67] The Irish Catholic clergy feared that ragged schools that had been opened by Protestant groups could now be given government support to establish themselves as reformatories and take in Catholic children and convert them. Paul Cullen wrote in a pastoral letter to be read in all Dublin churches that 'Lurgan-street, Townsend-street, the Coombe, and Rutland-street, are the seat of schools of this description'. From them, he wrote, agents were 'sent through the streets, to seize on poor neglected children, and to seduce them'.[68] In May, Meagher wrote again, thanking Cullen for his opinion on amendments which the chief secretary had introduced and urging him to arrange for petitions to be sent against the bill.[69]

Petitions against the proposed legislation had already begun to be circulated by John MacHale. On 14 February he had received a copy of the bill from 'one of the best and most faithful of the representatives of Ireland', possibly John Maguire. He called it 'anti-Catholic' and 'a Bill founded on Protestant religious instruction'. He issued a circular to the clergy of the diocese of Tuam on the same day, instructing them to have the petitions signed by their parishioners and 'transmitted by Sunday evening for presentation to the House of Commons'. In April the bishop of Clonfert, John Derry, and his clergy signed a petition at their synodical meeting. Not only did they object to the bill on the grounds that it facilitated the 'insulting annoyance of aggressive Protestant proselytism', they also complained that a long detention in a reformatory, disproportionate to the offence committed by a child, was unjust.[70]

On 19 May Horsman again brought an amended bill which stipulated that young offenders be sent to reformatories managed by 'Persons of the same Religious Persuasion' as themselves or their parents or guardians before the House of Commons.[71] The new bill did not satisfy some of the Catholic bishops and MPs. Patrick Joseph Murray wrote a public letter to the chief secretary stating that '[s]ome of our judges were of wonderfully active faith ... and ... many of them still cling to their old convictions and hatred of "Popery"'. He believed that sufficient money could not be gathered to found voluntary Catholic reformatories. While he supported integration in the national school system, he considered the reformatories to be different because, as Paul Sargent has noted when describing a later 'child-saving' organisation, '[s]aving the soul of the child and saving them from a life of crime [were] viewed as part of the same strategy'.[72] Citing Mary Carpenter and Matthew Davenport Hill to support his argument, Murray concluded by reminding the chief secretary of the work of Catholic agencies in the reformatory movements of France and Belgium and by asking him to '[c]onsider how cheaply and how cheerfully the agency of the Sisters of Mercy, of the Sisters of Charity, and of the Christian Brothers, could be brought to bear upon the Catholic juveniles in the course of their reformation'.[73] Petitions against the legislation from Catholic clergy and communities continued to arrive in London.[74] In June the annual synod of Irish bishops issued a pastoral letter which gave a clear instruction to MPs: 'We warn our representatives against the proposal before parliament for opening or assisting institutions for juvenile offenders.'[75] When asked in parliament the following year whether the government would introduce reformatory legislation for Ireland, Horsman responded that 'there was no reason to suppose that another Bill would be more acceptable' to the Irish members.[76]

Whether motivated by exasperation at the lack of legislative support, or in anticipation of it, a diverse group of people in Cork came together to establish Ireland's first juvenile reformatory on the principles that had been tried in other countries. In 1857 the Society of St Vincent de Paul became patrons of a proposed 'Home Agricultural Colony' for the delinquents of the city and county. Other patrons included the Catholic bishop of Cork, William Delany; Thomas O'Hagan, QC; Walter Berwick and John Maguire. Its president was Robert J. O'Shaughnessy. The colony was to be managed by Christian Brothers. Edmond Paul Townsend, a Presentation brother, and O'Shaughnessy embarked on an extensive tour of refuges, prisons and reformatories to observe their management. They visited Goldenbridge, Newgate and Mountjoy in Dublin, Mount St Bernard, Hammersmith and Belvedere Crescent in England, Mettray in France and Ruysselede in Belgium. In Mettray, the military discipline imposed on the boys left a strong impression on the Irish visitors:

I never shall forget being present when a family of the youngest children in the colony were going to bed – even in this they carried out their order and discipline. When the little fellows marched upstairs, they ranged themselves around the room, keeping up the military tramp. At the command 'a genoux' each was in one instant on his knees, and from a corner of the room came a weak, tiny voice beginning, *Notre pere, que es aux cieux*, the response of the fifty was spoken as if one voice, 'Ainsi'.[77]

They were more impressed with Ruysselede and felt this model should be used in Cork.[78] In spite of their head start, however, the proposed school did not open, and Cork would not have its own reformatory until July 1860.

In January 1858 Murray published a new draft bill in an article in the *Quarterly Review*, most of which had been prepared with the assistance of Walter Berwick. He reprinted the article – which also included objections to previous bills and detailed criminal statistics – in pamphlet form the following month. The new bill contained additional provisions for religious separation of the schools, and against institutions which had already been established being adapted as reformatories. Murray dedicated the pamphlet to the two judges, Thomas O'Hagan and Walter Berwick. Both had spoken in January in their charges to the grand juries of Dublin and Cork in support of the establishment of reformatories. While supporting the new institutions for criminal children, it is interesting to note that they did so in the context of relative peace and order in the country. O'Hagan, who had visited reformatories abroad, congratulated the grand jury in Kilmainham on the fact that 'the average annual criminality of Dublin [was] small'. They had each acknowledged the reduction in crime in the two cities, and the relatively peaceful state of the country as a whole.[79] In fact, they were acknowledging a dramatic diminution of crime for the period. In 1854 there had been 60,445 committals of prisoners to the county and town gaols in Ireland, of which 10,786, or 18 per cent, were children. By 1858, this number had fallen to 33,999 committals, of which 2,315, or 7 per cent, were children.[80] While most campaigners for the establishment of reformatory schools, in Ireland and abroad, cited rising numbers of criminal children to bolster their arguments for the need for the schools, the context was now very different in Ireland.

On 20 April 1858, Rickard Deasy, serjeant-at-law and MP for Cork, sought leave in the House of Commons to introduce a bill '[t]o promote and regulate Reformatory Schools for Juvenile Offenders in Ireland'.[81] He told his fellow MPs that 'large sums' of money had been collected in Cork for the establishment of a reformatory, but that the plan could not be advanced without the support of legislation. He noted that 'careful provision was made that no child should be sent to a school which was not under the exclusive management of persons of the same religious persuasion as the parents or guardians'. Lord Naas, who had replaced Horsman as chief secretary, told Deasy that, while he thought the bill worthy of consideration, the small number of children who had been sentenced in the higher courts in Ireland 'showed that the evil which his honourable and learned friend proposed to deal with was hardly of sufficient gravity to justify a special Act of Parliament'.[82]

Despite this and other objections, leave was granted and Deasy and John Bagwell, a Tipperary MP, presented the bill to parliament.[83] Lord Naas did not object to a second reading, but told the house that the bill would confer on magistrates 'a very extraordinary power – that of committing a mere child, for a very trivial offence, to an institution which was neither more nor less than a gaol', a comment which must have wounded the reformers who had devoted so much energy to removing children from gaols. Rickard Deasy's attempt to justify the need for reformatories in Ireland by quoting the English and Scottish figures, and the Irish statistics for 1856, did not work with the chief secretary. He knew, and retorted with, the number of juveniles sentenced at the assizes and quarter sessions in 1857 and asserted that the low incidence of juvenile crime in Ireland did not necessitate special measures, believing that proper separation in the gaols would suffice. It was Bagwell who defended the proposed legislation on this occasion, and it was agreed to move it to committee stage for amendments.[84]

Lord Naas objected to the manner in which the bill proposed to deal with how the schools should be funded. It provided for local authorities to contribute to both the buildings and the maintenance of the children, 'throw[ing] the whole cost of these establishments on the local rates'.[85] He was successful in having the bill amended so that the cost of buildings was removed. Further amendments were made on the manner in which courts could sentence children to reformatories.[86] A number of MPs objected to the section of the bill regarding religion, but John Maguire assured them that 'gentlemen of the strongest Protestant opinions in the south of Ireland were in favour of the separate system, and there was not the slightest fear that Protestant reformatories would not be established under this Bill'.[87] His assurance was not enough to convince everyone. When it reached the House of Lords, the earl of Clancarty spoke at length against it. A Galway landlord from the strongly evangelical Protestant family of Le Poer Trenches, he argued that very poor families would have their children commit crime to gain access to training and lodging in the reformatories, and that the legislation as it was proposed would ensure that the south and west of Ireland would only have Catholic reformatories.[88] It would be in Clancarty's home town of Ballinasloe that the province of Connacht's only reformatory, for Catholic girls, would be established.

Despite objections, and with amendments, the bill was finally granted royal assent on 2 August 1858. Under the new legislation, the chief secretary, on the advice of the inspector of prisons or such inspector as might be specially appointed, could certify a school on the application of its managers or directors, or withdraw such certification. Once a school was certified, a notice would be placed in the *Dublin Gazette* within the month, which would notify judges and magistrates that children could be sent to the institution. Funding could come from three main sources – the Treasury, grand juries and the parents of the child. Any child adjudged to be sixteen or under found guilty of an offence other than vagrancy at assizes, quarter sessions, Dublin Metropolitan Police courts, or petty sessions under the terms of the Summary Jurisdiction Act of 1851, could be sent to a reformatory at the expiration of their gaol sentence, which had to be one of at least fourteen days. The reformatory sentence enshrined by the act was for not less than one year and not more than five. Affirmation of Murray's great proviso of parental responsibility was included in section 15 of the act, which provided that parents 'of sufficient ability' should contribute up to five shillings' a week for the maintenance of their child while incarcerated, in default of which they could be imprisoned. A child who absconded would be imprisoned and then returned to the reformatory, and anyone abetting or harbouring an escapee would be fined up to £5. A form of probation was included in the act, whereby a child could be sent out to service to someone selected by the manager after they had served half their sentence and for a period of one year.[89] Like the English act, the new Irish Reformatories Act was permissive – it made it possible to establish reformatories and legally detain children in them, but judges and magistrates had complete discretion on how to dispose of a child found guilty of a crime.

While the legislation was being amended and debated, the Catholic Church in Ireland was going through a process of expansion and consolidation, with Archbishop Cullen leading the way. The period between 1851 and 1861 saw a 68 per cent increase in the number of nuns in the country,[90] with many European orders being introduced to Ireland by the Catholic hierarchy. The French order of Our Lady of Charity had opened a Magdalene asylum at High Park in Drumcondra in Dublin. The Dublin Catholic Reformatory Committee invited the sisters from this convent to open a school under the terms of the new legislation.[91] In December 1858, High Park was certified by the chief secretary as Ireland's first reformatory for Catholic girls.

The campaign to establish reformatories for criminal children in Ireland came at a time of great change. The effects of the Famine were waning, and the Catholic Church was growing in strength. While a religious contest was being waged for the souls of Ireland's poor, influential Catholics saw an opportunity to avail of government funding to create new institutions for the 'care and reformation' of young criminals. They succeeded in the face of powerful opposition.

Chapter 2

The First Reformatories

THE FIRST INSPECTOR OF REFORMATORIES was Walter Crofton. One of his duties was to make an annual report to parliament on the state of the new institutions. In his first report in 1862 Crofton wrote that there were 'only' nine reformatory schools. They held 513 inmates. He stated that he hoped to be able to publish information on the 'subsequent career' of discharged juveniles and on the development of the system in his next report.[1] He would not have that opportunity. Within a year he was replaced as inspector by Patrick Joseph Murray. This chapter will look at how the first reformatories evolved with regard to religion, funding, disciplinary structures and lived experience, and will assess the perceived successes and failures of the early years.

Religion: the 'be all and the end all' of reformation

In 1838 the then archbishop of Dublin, Daniel Murray, wrote to Paul Cullen that 'no rational person could entertain' the idea of state-funded denominational education for Catholics in Ireland.[2] Over the next twenty years Catholics steadily achieved positions of influence in the fields of education, politics and government administration. Patrick Joseph Murray was one of a growing number of Catholics who worked in senior positions in Dublin Castle.[3] He used the opportunity of his first report to parliament in 1863 to expound, at length, on his views on how the reformatory system had evolved and how it should develop in Ireland. He first reminded his readers of the obligation to send children to a reformatory managed by members of their, or their parents' or guardians', religion. This was the first of many reminders that were intended for the magistracy in particular. He praised the managers of the schools, writing that he had not detected any ill feeling towards them from the children, and that they were devoted 'heart and soul' to their work. He also wrote that Protestant and Catholic managers were co-operating and sharing information.[4]

Similar to High Park, the second reformatory to open was also for Catholic girls. The Sisters of Our Lady of Charity of the Good Shepherd had been invited to Limerick from France in the 1840s. Like the nuns in High Park, they managed a Magdalene asylum and they too opened a reformatory on the site of the asylum, which was certified on 25 January 1859.[5] The first manager of the school was Mrs Lockwood,[6] a nun who had founded the Dalbeth reformatory for girls in Glasgow.[7] The first Protestant school opened three months later at Cork Street in Dublin. It was certified on 12 April 1859 and was also for girls.[8] Unlike its Catholic counterparts, Cork Street was under lay management. Miss Cooke, who had experience working in the convict prisons, was the matron, and she was assisted by Miss Sharpe. A management committee established and supervised the school, and its secretary, Rev. Shore, also acted as chaplain. He was, in addition, chaplain to the convict prisons. The marks system used in the prisons, whereby inmates could earn extra privileges for good behaviour, was replicated in Cork Street.[9]

Of all the schools that opened after the passing of the Reformatory Schools (Ireland) Act, it was the school for Catholic boys at Glencree which garnered the most public attention, thanks to its influential fundraising committee and its secretary, Patrick Joseph Murray. A site was chosen in a mountainous area in County Wicklow, leased from Lord Powerscourt, and the school was certified on the same day as Cork Street.[10] The male religious order of Oblates was chosen for the management of the school. It was the first boys' reformatory to open. In June 1860 Archbishop Cullen visited the school and one hundred boys took confirmation, an event which one newspaper described as 'one of the most potent illustrations of the influences of religion for good'.[11]

The school was not universally praised, however. Public criticisms of Glencree were made by members of the Protestant community. A letter to the editor of the *Irish Times and Daily Advertiser* in 1860 was titled 'New Mode of Kidnapping – Reformatory Schools'. Its author, 'Clericus', told the story of a fourteen-year-old boy named James Tyrrell who was sent to Glencree. His parents were Protestant, but he had told the court that he was Catholic.[12] Tyrrell's case and that of a boy called William Hawthorne were described by Rev. Richard Smyth in a long pamphlet which was highly critical of the reformatory system in Ireland. Hawthorne was also a Protestant boy who was sent to Glencree. Appeals were sent to the lord lieutenant to have the children sent to Protestant reformatories. Hawthorne's parents were said to have received eloquent letters from him describing

Glencree as a 'capital school', although he was recorded as illiterate when he went there. He later denied writing the letters and said that they had been written by a member of staff at Glencree. Smyth's pamphlet alleged that staff at Richmond bridewell were convincing boys that if they declared themselves Catholic and were sent to Glencree they would have 'meat three times a week; have a band of music, foot-ball, &c., and the free run of the mountains'.[13]

In its early years the manager of the school, Rev. Francis J. Lynch, was also criticised for refusing admission to some boys. The reasons varied. Boys who were considered unsuitable for the harsh climate and hard work were turned away, as were boys whose sentences were considered too short, at two or three years. This caused friction with members of the judiciary and the prison authorities. Smyth cited the recorder of Dublin, in his charge to the grand jury, saying that he 'had to guard [his] own judicial sentences from being set aside by a *private and irresponsible tribunal*, however respectable and well-intentioned'.[14] Boys were also refused if he considered that their crimes were too serious. During a meeting held at the Music Hall in Dublin, Lynch had said that Glencree was to be a school for 'reclaiming and reforming boys convicted of minor offences'.[15] Richard Smyth wrote that Glencree 'must have good boys or none'.[16]

A reformatory at Goldenbridge was certified in May 1859[17] and was intended for older Dublin girls. A reformatory for adults had existed in Goldenbridge before the opening of the juvenile institution. As part of the marks, or 'intermediate' system, well-behaved female Catholic prisoners from Mountjoy convict prison could be sent to a refuge run by the Sisters of Mercy in Goldenbridge. It had been opened by Archbishop Cullen in 1856.[18] While the adult reformatory was deemed by most observers to be a great success, its juvenile branch was less successful and destined to become Ireland's shortest-lived reformatory school. When Walter Crofton visited the school in 1861 – and he noted that it had been 'constantly visited' by him – he observed that 'the most shameless and abandoned of Dublin young criminals' were sent there. He also believed some of them to be over the age of sixteen, which was in contravention of the Reformatory Schools Act. They were engaged in laundry work and sewing.[19] The manager of the school, Mrs Kirwan, a Mercy nun, was described by the American penal reformer E.C. Wines as 'brimful of genius, heart, energy, enthusiasm, good sense' and he confessed himself to be 'spell-bound in her presence' after a visit to the adult reformatory.[20]

Shortly after the passing of the Reformatory Schools Act in 1858, an influential group of people began to plan for a school for Ulster Catholic girls. The bishop of Clogher; the mother of Lady Rossmore, who was a Catholic convert; Monaghan native and prison inspector John Lentaigne; and Ellen Woodlock, whose family owned the woollen mills at Blarney, decided to open a reformatory in the town of Monaghan. Ellen Woodlock had recruited girls for the St Louis order in Juilly in France. One of these was Priscilla Beale, an English convert to Catholicism. The bishop wrote to France for a foundation of the St Louis order to be established in Monaghan, beginning with a reformatory. Three sisters arrived there on 6 January 1859. They had expected to find a building ready for them but had to wait until Charles Bianconi provided funds for the purchase of a defunct brewery at Spark's Lake.[21] It was certified on 3 May.[22] Priscilla, now Sr Genevieve, became its manager.

By late 1859 there was, as yet, no Protestant reformatory for boys. This situation would soon change. Rehoboth Place was established for Protestant boys in Dublin and was the last of six schools which were certified in 1859. It was set up by the same committee that founded the Cork Street school, and, like Cork Street, was under lay management. It was managed day-to-day by Thomas Hanna, and Rev. Shore oversaw its running on behalf of the committee.

The next school to open after Rehoboth was also for Protestant boys. The Malone school in Belfast was certified in March 1860, and, like Glencree, initially had a large and influential fundraising committee of clerics, members of the judiciary and interested members of the public. The school was established on the outskirts of the city and had twenty-three acres of land attached to it.[23] At the committee's second annual meeting in Belfast Town Hall, the Protestant bishop of Down, Connor and Dromore took the chair and, much to the alarm of those present, while praising the Malone school, began to list alleged abuses and faults with the reformatory system. In particular, he raised the issues of the lack of inspection, the cost of the system and the argument that it gave a 'premium to crime' to poor or negligent parents and their children. He was challenged on these allegations by William Tracey, a magistrate who claimed that he was responsible for sending all but one or two of its inmates to Malone. Tracey spoke of boys who appeared before him in court, having already been in gaol, and who said to him, 'What am I to do? My hair is cut; everybody knows that I have come from prison, and nobody will employ me; I must steal or die'. Tracey told the meeting that he had got some of these boys into the workhouse, but they had left, becoming 'tired of the monotony of workhouse life'. He believed that a reformatory was the best place that he, as a magistrate, could send such boys.[24]

After two years of planning and fundraising, the Cork Catholic reformatory for boys opened at Upton in July 1860. It was the only Irish reformatory school to be purpose-built. It was designed to accommodate 160 boys and had 112 acres of land attached to it. The Cork reformatory committee chose the Rosminian order to take over the day-to-day management of the school. The order had been running a reformatory in Yorkshire.[25] They appointed Rev. Moses Furlong as manager. Shortly after the opening of the school he wrote to Murray expressing his frustration at what he perceived to be the low number of boys being sent there. At the same time, he was informed that 'the city and county of Cork abound with young "Arabs", leading a life of crime, and growing up hardened criminals'. Neither Murray nor Furlong were in any doubt as to where the blame lay. Some magistrates were not sending enough, or any, children to the school.

Furlong cited a number of examples of children whose cases appeared in the local papers and who were not sent to Upton. 'A good and worthy magistrate' had told him that he was on the point of sending three boys to the school but had given in to the 'entreaties and promises on the part of the parents' and had dismissed the case instead.[26]

Connacht was the last province to have a reformatory. In December 1863 Mary Burke, the superior of the Mercy convent in Ballinasloe, County Galway, wrote to the chief secretary, Robert Peel, that she had been 'for some time past ... preparing, and ha[d] now nearly completed the buildings and fittings of a proposed reformatory for Roman Catholic girls: an institution much needed in the Province'.[27] She was acting 'under the direction and patronage' of Dr Derry,[28] the bishop, who, in 1856 had organised a petition against the reformatories. Murray inspected the premises and found that the sisters were 'fully prepared to receive twelve children, and [had] the complete school uniform, with beds, bedding, and bed clothing for that number'.[29] The school was certified in February 1864. Although the girls were 'happily placed' and in receipt of the 'devoted attention' of the sisters, Murray was again disappointed with the response of the provincial judiciary. Mary Burke had 'given full intimation to all concerned that the school was open', and Murray had sent an official notification to the magistrates.[30] At the Galway spring assizes the following month, the judges did not appear to have noted it in their charges to the jury, an occasion which they usually used to summarise 'the state of the county' or town regarding matters judicial and criminal. A number of young girls appeared at Galway courts after the opening of the reformatory and were not sent to the new school. Even as late as April 1865, an eleven-year-old boy named John Egan had to be discharged after a Galway magistrate sentenced him to the girls' reformatory for five years for stealing eggs.[31] The lack of engagement with, and knowledge of, the new institutions amongst the magistracy was a source of great frustration for the inspector.

Paul Sargent has written that 'Murray saw the principles of Catholic teaching as playing a central role in the work of the reformatory schools'.[32] As Murray himself wrote, 'religion must be made the be all and the end all of every hope of Reformation'.[33] The Irish reformatory system was established with strict demarcation between Protestant and Catholic and the legislation was shaped to facilitate this. The speed with which the Catholic clergy established schools meant that by 1870 there were ten reformatories, seven of which were for Catholic children, and Murray's successor wrote of overcrowding in the Catholic schools for boys.[34] The day-to-day management of the Catholic schools was carried out by religious orders, and the new institutions and the funding they received formed part of the financial framework of a Catholic Church that was growing in size and confidence under the direction of Archbishop Cullen. This perceived 'colonisation' of childcare[35] alarmed some members of the Protestant community but laid the foundations for a system of childcare that would last for over a century.

The 'cost to the nation': funding the system

Income for the schools came from five possible sources. The first was from voluntary contributions, though Murray was disappointed with the lack of public support which the schools received in Ireland. The industrial labour of the children acted as a second source of income for some of the reformatories but much of their work was in the upkeep of the schools. A third source, and one which Murray pushed and promoted from the outset, came from the parents of the inmates. He believed that it was important to enforce parental contributions in order to deter unscrupulous parents from deliberately having their children sent to reformatories, and to punish parents whose neglect led their children to commit crime. Of the 591 children in reformatories in 1862, 228 had both parents living, 253 had just one parent alive and 110 were orphans. In Dublin, John Ryan, a collector, was appointed to visit the parents and collect the money. Between 1860 and 1862 he issued 124 warrants for non-payment and nine parents were sent to gaol.[36] A fourth source of income came from the local authorities of the areas the children came from. Murray believed that, since they were relieved of the burden of maintaining the children in their gaols, they should contribute. The payment was discretionary, however, and some local authorities did not pay. The fifth and main source of income for the schools was a grant from the Treasury. Initially 5s per week per child, this was raised to 7s in 1862 'at the urgent request of the managers' but lowered to 6s later that year.[37]

Richard Smyth believed that the reformatory system was placing too heavy a financial burden on the country. In a section of his pamphlet entitled 'Cost to the Nation' he compared the cost of keeping a child in a reformatory with the workhouse system: 'What pauper child will thank you for your paltry £6 a year when, by stealing an apple or a pair of shoes, he can compel you to support him, like a boy of patrician rank, in a first-rate academy, at the rate of £28 per annum?'[38] Supporters of the reformatories argued that by intercepting the nascent criminal career of a child and training that child to earn an honest living, society was saved from having to deal with a long life of crime.

Large and well-publicised meetings were held in Dublin to promote the work that was being done in Glencree and to raise money for the improvement and enlargement of the buildings, most of which had been built for the cavalry at the end of the eighteenth century and had been largely unused since then. The *Irish Quarterly Review* described the meeting in the Music Hall in 1859 as a 'numerous and highly respectable meeting of citizens of Dublin', with a number of ladies occupying 'places in the boxes',[39] but *The Irish Times* reported that '[t]he attendance in the body of the hall was not numerous'.[40] The same could not be said of the platform, with more than sixty men – clerics, judges, politicians and government officials – occupying seats at the front of the hall. The school's director, Fr Lynch, reported that thirteen boys had been sent to the school since it opened in April. He put two proposals to the meeting. The first, and his and the committee's preferred option, was that new buildings should be erected adjacent to the existing ones to accommodate 'many hundreds of boys', to equal or be bigger than any reformatory school in Britain or Ireland. The second option involved the renovation of the existing dilapidated buildings to accommodate eighty to a hundred boys. The meeting passed a motion, proposed by the provincial of the Oblates, that the committee should appoint collectors to raise funds for the school. A list of subscriptions was read to the meeting by Patrick Joseph Murray.[41] In the next two years the school took in more children than any other. When Walter Crofton visited Glencree on 18 October 1861, he found that there were 239 boys detained there. 'I trust', he wrote, 'that the number of inmates in this school will not be increased'. Crofton's experience of reformatories convinced him that smaller numbers and the 'family system' used in continental and British schools were more effective in the treatment and future disposal of juvenile criminals.[42]

By the mid-1860s Glencree faced a financial crisis. The school still lacked adequate buildings and had a debt of £4,000. The public support which it had courted did not materialise. In 1863 it received £3,972 from the Treasury and only £32 from subscriptions.[43] The school became increasingly dependent on the capitation grant. Smyth and others criticised the government funding as excessive compared with the cost of maintenance in other institutions and warned that it could lead to the incarceration of relatively innocent children for the sake of the grant.[44] In his first visit to the school as inspector in 1870, John

Lentaigne found the building 'much overcrowded', and noted that at one point there had been 366 boys incarcerated there.[45]

By the end of 1862 Upton was home to 147 boys but in 1866 there were 121 boys in the school and seventy 'vacancies'. The result, Furlong said, was that the school was 'no longer self-supporting'.[46] The pressure to fill Upton would appear to have influenced the chances of children leaving. John Walsh had been found guilty of conspiracy to cheat and defraud his employer, the local priest, at Ballinamore, County Leitrim, in 1864. He was sent to Upton. Three years later, in the same year that Furlong was writing to Murray about the low numbers in his school, John Walsh's father appealed to the lord lieutenant to have his son released early. John's sister had paid for his passage to America, and his father's memorial contained proof of purchase of the ticket and was endorsed by the local magistrate and the priest who had accused the boy of the crime. Furlong refused to let him go, stating that he was one of the best-behaved boys in the school, had reached the position of 'sergeant-major' and was 'an extremely clever' carpenter. By his own admission, Walsh would appear to have been 'reformed' and was an ideal case for release on licence. It is probable that the value of the boy's labour and the capitation he brought in for an undersubscribed school kept him incarcerated.[47] John Lentaigne asked the schools to send him regular reports identifying children who were eligible for release on licence. He frequently admonished the managers for not doing so, telling the Upton managers that 'the child's parents had a right to him', but he had no power to compel them to release the boys. In 1883 the secretary of Upton conceded that, in some cases, there might be a tendency to keep older boys 'whose labour was most remunerative'.[48]

By the end of the 1860s only one school, Malone in Belfast, had more inmates than the numbers Murray was claiming they could accommodate. It is not known whether the number that he included in his annual reports as 'capacity' for each of the schools was one imposed by him or by the school managers, and this number changed from year to year.

Reformatory	Number of inmates	Capacity
Malone	64	60
Upton	140	160
Rehoboth	40	60
Glencree	309	350
Ballinasloe	17	25
Cork Street	16	25
High Park	40	45
Limerick	34	50
Spark's Lake	41	60
Total	701	835

Table 1: Inmates in reformatories, 1869[49]

By 1870 Upton was at full capacity, with an average of 207 inmates,[50] and Furlong was refusing entry to new boys, two of whom were Bernard Young and William McKinny. The manager of Glencree agreed to take Young even though his school was also overcrowded but refused McKinny because he 'had not sufficient bodily strength to undergo labour'. William McKinny, who was fifteen years old and only three feet ten in height, hanged himself in Belfast gaol a year later. Bernard Young died in a snowstorm while being escorted through the mountains to Glencree. He had been sent from Belfast gaol without shoes or stockings. In an act of extraordinary bravery, the prison officer who was sent to escort him carried Bernard on his back through the snow and wind and refused to leave him while help was sought. Bernard died in the officer's arms.[51]

Cork Street was not a big school, with an average of about eight to fifteen girls being held there. The annual report of the committee that oversaw the school reported in 1865 that '[t]he profits to be realised by industrial work can never, in a Reformatory School, be in proportion to the number of inmates'.[52] The purpose of the schools was to train the children in work which would make them 'industrious citizens who would be reintegrated into the community'.[53] With regard to the training which was carried out in the schools for girls, Murray cited Mary Carpenter in his first report. She had written that reformatories should 'aim to prepare our girls for domestic service'.[54] The Cork Street girls worked at needlework and contributed to the upkeep of the house through painting, wallpapering and glazing. Matthew Davenport Hill and his daughter visited Cork Street and noted that the girls also made the underclothes for the Protestant boys' reformatory. They were impressed to note that two girls were absent while they were visiting, shopping for food for the school, and that such girls were entrusted with money.[55]

In its early years the girls in Limerick were put to work at shirt-making, laundry work and lacemaking. The latter was introduced by Mother Mary of St Louis de Baligand, a Bavarian aristocrat, and taught by Emilie van Verevenhaven, a Belgian laywoman.[56] The making of lace did not bring any profit and the laundry was extended. Walter Crofton was pleased to note that, in its early years, the girls were to be given a gratuity for the work they did, something he believed would help them associate industry with profit.[57] The school was also initially supported by some of the gentry of County Limerick. A number of buildings were erected at the front of the convent for the reformatory and the inspector was anxious that the reformatory girls should have no opportunity to see or in any way communicate with the Magdalene women who were housed behind the convent. In 1870, John Lentaigne, who replaced Murray as inspector, could report that the profits from the laundry were 'considerable'. Although it was the sixth largest reformatory in the country at the time in terms of numbers of inmates, it was bringing in the largest profit – £307 in one year.[58]

By 1870, there were 856 children in ten Irish reformatories. They cost £18,275 to run. Just over £1,000 was received through voluntary contributions from the public, a sum which John Lentaigne noted was 'far in excess of that in either of the previous years'.[59] Local authorities contributed £5,248 for the upkeep of children from their areas. The labour of the children brought in £984. The work of the boys in Rehoboth represented £3 11s per child whereas the manager of Glencree, which by 1870 had 325 inmates, reported a loss of over 6s per child. By far the most successful school in terms of profit from the labour of the children was Limerick, where the girls were generating £7 14s per head, 'mostly from laundry and needlework'. The Treasury grant continued to be the main source of income for the reformatories, representing over £12,000 of the total receipts for 1870.[60] While financial matters were becoming a pressing concern for those responsible for the administration of the schools, the disciplinary structures of each of the reformatories were evolving differently as school managers sometimes struggled to deal with the reality of life in the new institutions.

Leg bolts and blue ribbons: discipline

In Walter Crofton's convict prisons inmates could progress through a classification system whereby they earned privileges for good behaviour. In some of the reformatories children could also earn marks and they could be translated into extra advantages or money which would be saved for when they left the reformatory. Echoing the principles of Jeremy Bentham's panopticon, and reflecting the system used in Mettray, Murray wrote that great care was taken that the children were always within sight, hearing and 'complete control' of those in charge,[61] facilitating what Paul Sargent has described as a 'process of internalisation of moral values'.[62] This type of 'total institution', where every aspect of an inmate's life was controlled, was believed to be the most effective path to reformation.[63] Regarding discipline, Murray suggested that deprivation of food and 'working in solitude' be used as punishment. While allowing for certain freedoms for the new managers in the way that they ran their schools, he reserved for himself the right to insist that they observe rules which he set out in his first report.[64] As the schools evolved, they each developed different disciplinary structures.

In 1861 Fr Lynch outlined to a meeting in Dublin the disciplinary regime at Glencree, a system that went much further than restricted diet and working alone. He noted that there existed amongst the young inmates a 'latent, lurking disposition to steal', mostly food. The system of discipline was based on that of the Calder Farm school in Yorkshire. The boys were divided into three sections – the section of honour, the section of reserve and the section of disgrace. A boy found guilty of a serious fault was made to wear a 'black dress' and was 'debarred from association' with other boys. If the bad behaviour continued, the boy had to kneel at mealtimes in the refectory, where he was fed on bread and water. In the words of the director, 'he is sure to be humbled and subdued after one or two weeks' of this treatment. Boys in the section of honour were better fed, better clothed, could earn up to a shilling a week, and could be promoted to the rank of 'sergeant'. There were thirteen boys classed as 'sergeant', and they, he said, assisted the staff in 'the maintenance of order'.[65] A similar system of military discipline was used in Mettray, where it became the 'dominant characteristic' of a regime in which each boy was expected to 'see himself as a soldier who must submit to authority'.[66] When the delegation from Cork had visited the French school, they were told that everything was done with military precision, 'to sound of trumpet'.[67] A former soldier who had served in India trained the Glencree boys in military drill, training which it was hoped would assist them in finding work in the army when they were released. Eighteen Glencree boys enlisted in 1863 and 1864. In 1865 Murray wrote in his annual report that the manager of the school was 'never without a military guard of honour' during furlough season, and that he himself sometimes had a 'red-coated visitor' to his office in Dublin.[68]

Richard Smyth attacked almost every aspect of the system in Glencree, including its disciplinary structure. He described reformatories as no different to prisons where children were sent for the best years of their lives for trivial offences, and where they would be put to work blasting rocks. He quoted Fr Lynch's description of the punishments meted out to boys in the section of disgrace and wrote, 'If an inmate of a reformatory is maltreated ... what redress has he?' He compared reformatories negatively with gaols, where inspectors, chaplains, doctors and a board of superintendence could be appealed to by prisoners who felt they had been mistreated. The infrequent visits of the inspector to the schools were not, he believed, sufficient to ensure the safety of the children.

'We tremble to think', he wrote, 'of the abuses that may in course of time creep into these establishments.'[69]

Smyth and other critics of Glencree would find themselves facing a formidable opponent. In the late 1860s Fr Lynch was replaced as manager by Lawrence Charles Prideaux Fox, an English Quaker convert to Catholicism. Fr Fox had gained a great deal of notoriety in 1860 when, as chaplain of the South Dublin Union workhouse, he had intervened when some young female inmates complained that they had been searched by male staff for stolen goods. Attempts to have him sacked resulted in the intervention of Archbishop Cullen and the issue was raised in the House of Commons.[70]

E.C. Wines visited Glencree in the early 1870s in the company of John Lentaigne. He described Fr Fox as 'the right man in the right place'. He was less impressed with the location of the reformatory and was critical of the exposed location which gave rise to 'intense' cold in winter, and of the bad land, most of which he described as irreclaimable.[71] Wines was in Europe having organised the First International Congress on the Prevention and Repression of Crime in London. He visited prisons and reformatories throughout the continent and spent two days in Mettray. He told Frédéric-Auguste Demetz that he had 'created the best reformatory in the world'. One of the key aspects of Mettray to which its success was attributed was the fact that, although it held almost eight hundred 'colons' (inmates), the 'family system' was maintained whereby boys lived in houses of fifty, supervised by a 'chef de famille' and an assistant.[72] Wines seemed unperturbed by the overcrowding in Glencree and expressed satisfaction at being told that 'ninety per cent of [the boys] are reformed and, on their liberation, become a constituent part of the industrious and honest yeomanry of the country'.[73] In England at the time only one of the thirty-six reformatories for boys held more than 300 children.[74]

Problems of discipline, although largely unreported by Murray, began to emerge in High Park. John Lentaigne told a government enquiry that he had been 'astonished' to discover that his predecessor had brought straps and leg bolts to High Park to restrain the girls.[75] Absconding was dealt with harshly, both for the children and those who sheltered them. The school's closeness to Dublin facilitated escape. The full rigour of the section of the Reformatory Schools Act which provided for prosecution of anyone harbouring an escapee was enforced as a warning to others. One woman served a two-month sentence in Grangegorman prison for concealing her son after he absconded from Glencree.[76] When Julia Connolly ran away from High Park some time later, it was her parents who brought her back. Murray wrote that the provision of the act was 'now well known to those parents whose children are under detention in Reformatory Schools'.[77] Disciplinary problems at High Park escalated to such an extent that by the early 1870s many girls had been transferred from the school to other reformatories.

In Goldenbridge the energy and genius of Mrs Kirwan that had so impressed E.C. Wines would appear to have failed her when faced with young Dublin girls. Crofton wrote that the 'reckless and abandoned character' of some of the girls 'very sadly taxes the energy' of the manager.[78] She wrote to Paul Cullen in 1861 about one girl, Rose, who had been a workhouse inmate and was sent to Goldenbridge. Her bad behaviour in the reformatory earned her a prison sentence after three months. Mrs Kirwan told the archbishop that months later they were still trying to eradicate the evil influence which Rose had over the other inmates.[79] Rose was fourteen years old and had been brought to the South Dublin workhouse by her aunt for treatment for venereal disease, a condition Rose claimed was the result of a sexual assault by a man who was chairman of Naas Town Council and deputy chairman of Naas Board of Guardians.[80]

Murray ordered the transfer of seven of the thirty-four Goldenbridge inmates to other schools because of their refractory behaviour. After the transfer, they became 'tractable and quiet'. He praised the work that Mrs Kirwan had done with the other girls and reported that, because some of the discharged girls came from the 'worst' kind of families, she obtained £90 to assist them to emigrate.[81] It is not clear why Goldenbridge presented such a challenge to a manager who had experience of working with adult offenders. When Fanny Taylor visited High Park in 1867, a nun there told her that 'work with the children was far, far more arduous and discouraging than that with the women'.[82] It may also have been that Mrs Kirwan was pressurised into opening the school – Murray wrote that she was 'induced' to do so.[83]

Five of the transferred Goldenbridge girls were sent to the Spark's Lake reformatory in Monaghan. By 1862, Murray was writing that the Monaghan school was receiving 'some of the most vicious and refractory girls' he had ever seen[84] and effecting transformations in their behaviour which the *Freeman's Journal* called 'something short of miracles'.[85] Murray later said of Sr Genevieve that:

> Were it not for the Manager's (Mrs Beale) indomitable perseverance in her mission, and her courage in accepting the transfer from High Park of the worst class of Dublin girls, eight at the least would have been thrown upon the world and into utter depravity. There are none so wicked, so violent – so, to all human judgement, lost – as to be beyond the scope of her zeal and sympathy.[86]

The girls who were incarcerated in the Monaghan school were segregated into two groups. All new admissions were kept completely separate from the 'class of honour' in a probationary class. Only in the 'class of honour' did the girls enjoy recreation and secular education.[87] The girls were 'never idle, and yet never over-worked'.[88] To this Murray attributed the successful disciplinary regime of the school. By 1871 John Lentaigne was referring to Spark's Lake as a 'penal reformatory school', where girls who were considered incorrigible in other schools were sent.[89]

Notwithstanding the strict regime in Monaghan, problems arose. In 1864 the inspector called for the intervention of the chief secretary when three girls absconded. On Christmas Day, Teresa Cushlahan [Cushnahan], Mary Myles and Margaret Brady escaped. Five days later they surrendered themselves to a police station near Cavan. Murray wrote to the chief secretary arguing that if the girls were transferred to another reformatory, the other inmates would consider it a 'triumph' and a 'victory over the manager'. The girls were given gaol sentences of between three and nine months with hard labour.[90]

Rehoboth used the marks system, a regime which Murray believed had the effect that 'each boy knows that his position in the Reformatory depends entirely on himself'. Thomas Hanna initially managed the school alone, with the help of monitors selected from the inmates. In the larger Protestant reformatory for boys in Belfast, problems of discipline were also occurring. Malone was first managed by a Mr Falconer who, like Mrs Lockwood in Limerick, had reformatory experience in Glasgow.[91] There were frequent abscondings from Malone, and Patrick Joseph Murray wrote to the school's committee 'recommending certain modifications in the management'. By 1862, Falconer had left to work in an English reformatory and the committee appointed David Barclay, who had been in Rehoboth, in his place. As in the Dublin school, the boys worked at cultivating the land, tailoring and shoemaking.[92] In 1864 the average number of inmates was around forty, and overcrowding meant that Mr Barclay had to be very vigilant to ensure that 'no evil arose'.[93]

In only one Irish reformatory did the manager state that corporal punishment was eschewed. By 1870, Ballinasloe had reached capacity, with twenty-five inmates, although John Lentaigne noted that it was capable of taking more girls. He regarded the school as a success in its treatment of its inmates. He attributed this success to the fact that the nuns never left the girls, day or night. Mary Burke explained the disciplinary regime at the school:

> Any corporal chastisement hardens and degrades. The system of marks is the most powerful agent for reformation, and red, green and blue ribbons are worn by the different classes.[94]

It is remarkable that Ballinasloe chose not to use violence as a disciplinary tool for its inmates at a time when beating of children was commonplace in all types of schools, and continued to be used until well into the twentieth century.[95] The extent of corporal punishment used in the other schools would only become known in the early 1880s when a government enquiry required reformatory managers to submit details of the punishments meted out to the children. They recorded lashes, strokes of straps and canes, whipping, solitary confinement and bread and water diets as part of their disciplinary arsenal.[96] While the systems of discipline used in the schools could be used as a form of punishment, they also served another purpose – namely to impose a regularity and routine on daily life in the institutions.

Regularity and resistance: daily life

Patrick Joseph Murray described the regime in the schools in his first report as follows:

> The rule in all the Schools is steady, hard work; a dietary plain and wholesome, but such as hard work requires – a dietary such as children reared as these children have been, and tainted as most of them are with scrofulous tendency, renders necessary; this is just the kind of food they receive, and such as every Manager of a School considers himself bound to give, unless he will break faith with the public, and render his School a hospital, not a Reformatory.

There should be no attempt, he instructed, to make scholars of the inmates; rather, 'habits of industry, regularity, self-denial, self-reliance, and self-control' should be inculcated in them. The children's day would begin at six in the morning, and end at eight in the evening, with seven hours of work and three hours of schooling punctuated by three meals, prayer and play. Murray wrote that he had seen 'no downcast looks' amongst the children and found them to be 'candid, honest and open in manner'.[97]

For many of the children sent to reformatories the order and discipline was in stark contrast to the chaos of their daily lives on the outside. A large number of the boys who were sent to the Malone reformatory in Belfast came from the notorious Anderson's Row, a short street of about twelve buildings, a 'miasma of rotten straw, filthy rags, and rubbish of every description' and a 'nursery for young criminals'. Julius Rodenberg visited it in 1860 and wrote of a female Fagin, 'an old stout woman [who] ... keeps several young women, by whom the boys are utterly corrupted in an unnatural way; they are instructed how to pilfer in the streets and in the port, and seduce other boys by representations and promises to Anderson-row'. Rodenberg was told that three-quarters of the inmates of Belfast's reformatory and gaol had come from the little cul-de-sac.[98] William Hawthorne and Teresa Cushnahan had been living in Anderson's Row before being sentenced together by William Tracey for stealing cloth.[99]

When Moses Furlong wrote to Murray about the 'vacancies' in his reformatory he gave details of young boys who had been convicted of multiple thefts in Cork city, some of whom claimed that their parents drank or were neglectful.[100] Not all of the children came from backgrounds of poverty. While it has been argued that the purpose of the reformatories was the 'regulation of the poor' and control of the poorer classes,[101] records from the early years of the system reveal a wide range of parental occupations of the first inmates. These include a policeman, a whitesmith, apothecaries, a governess, doctors and an attorney.[102]

Matthew Davenport Hill and his daughter visited High Park in 1865 and described how the nuns had taken the 'rough material' from their 'mud hovels' and taught them to 'use their fingers deftly'. They described their first sight of the girls:

We found them assembled in the schoolroom, and, though among the countenances before us were some striking examples of Irish beauty and sprightliness, the majority bore marks of degraded parentage and vicious habits. Among the latter a little creature was pointed out to us who came to the School last winter. The morning after her arrival she was found cowering over the fire by one of the nuns, who asked if anything ailed her. She answered, 'Yes, but a glass of spirits would make me all right.' Her relatives on both sides, to the third and fourth degree, are inmates of the convict prisons.[103]

Mary Burke wrote of the reaction of children when they arrived in Ballinasloe:

When a child first enters the institution she is generally awed by the strictness and regularity which she sees around, and has sufficient cunning to conceal her natural propensities, and it is only after some time, when her true character is developed, that reformation begins.

In March 1864 Ballinasloe received its first inmate, Margaret Seery. Margaret had been convicted in Sligo, along with her mother, for stealing five shillings'. She was ten years old and had been born in the workhouse. The inspector of prisons reported that Margaret's mother was an 'inveterate thief' who had trained Margaret to steal.[104] She was entering a small, enclosed world. By December, there were only six girls in Ballinasloe.[105] The girls worked at laundry and needlework and were trained to be servants. Their schooling would appear to have been slightly broader than in most other schools and was based on the national school system. In Monaghan, the nuns had received their first reformatory child on 14 October 1859. Ellen Brown was an eleven-year-old girl from Belfast who had seven convictions prior to her reformatory sentence. Sr Genevieve wrote of her that she 'presented a pale and emaciated appearance, from the habitual use of strong liquors, during the short periods when in the enjoyment of liberty, and owing to the rigours of a refractory cell, while undergoing punishment in a gaol'.[106]

By the end of 1864, High Park held fifty girls and had a staff of six. For the first years, the sisters and children 'had to make do with the outhouses of the kitchen yard for schoolroom, refectory and dormitory'.[107] Murray described the buildings as 'very plain, but well ventilated'.[108] Most of the girls who were sent to the school had been sentenced by the Dublin courts. Murray wrote that the nun who managed the school, Mary O'Callaghan, had gained a great deal of experience in dealing with 'town-reared girls' while in France. Although originally intended for younger Dublin female criminals, by 1864 the school was taking what the inspector described as 'an extremely vicious and hardened class of girls'.[109] The literary education of the girls in High Park was described by Murray as 'sufficient'. Their training in needlework, laundry work, baking and the duties of a general servant was praised. Three inmates of the school were permitted to make shirts and stockings for their brothers who were inmates in Glencree reformatory, and the brothers made shoes for their sisters.[110]

The proximity of High Park to Dublin city allowed for access to the inmates by family and friends. Parents and family members who were considered to be of reputable character were permitted to visit them once a quarter, but only if the child's behaviour had been good, and under close supervision. Murray described the importance of such visits:

> The child ... recollects what she was; she knows what she is; she talks of her past and her present to her parent or friend; perhaps the lady who has charge joins in the conversation, and thus, in many cases, through the instrumentality of a poor child-criminal, the heart of a parent or a friend has been taught to think of God forgotten, and of religion neglected.[111]

In the Cork Street reformatory the Davenport Hills were impressed with the order and cleanliness which they saw:

> The house was exquisitely clean – the boards as white as could be – every article of metal polished to the utmost brilliancy; the beds were perfectly arranged, and lying upon each was a brush and comb and small toothcomb as clean as when they came from the shop ... in fact, the house throughout looked like none we ever saw before, except in Holland; and this, remember, is in Ireland![112]

Their literary education was good and Murray considered it to be 'one of the most perfect Reformatory Schools' he had ever visited.[113] In 1866 he noted that not one of the girls who served a full term in the school had relapsed into crime, even though some of the girls were 'as vicious and depraved as it was possible for persons of their age to be'.[114] Tahaney Alghrani argues that '[t]he ideals of "respectable femininity" were deeply integrated and embedded' in the running of schools for girls in England,[115] and these ideals are also reflected in the aspirations of managers and inspectors of Irish schools.

In the boys' schools the majority of inmates worked outdoors. In Upton most of the boys worked at reclaiming land and growing agricultural produce. The city of Cork and town of Bandon were easily accessible and the reformatory had a railway station on the grounds. It was hoped that sale of the produce would bring in a profit for the school. Some of the boys were trained in tailoring, shoemaking and carpentry, and a band was formed.[116] Murray made a rare criticism of the school in 1865 when he questioned the standard of the literary education of the boys,[117] but he subsequently reported it to be satisfactory. When the Davenport Hills visited Glencree in July 1865, they found boys reclaiming 'a hill of stones', blasting boulders, and working at trades and the upkeep of the house, including manufacturing their own gas. The boys, although dirty, were perceived as superior in health and cheerfulness to the boys at Ruysselede or Mettray and entertained their visitors with a band performance of 'God Save the Queen' and 'St Patrick's Day'.[118]

Patrick Joseph Murray's rather benign portrayals of life in the institutions, however, cannot be taken at face value. His reports as inspector predominantly presented the reformatories in a very positive light. As a result, a clear picture of the extent of resistance and insubordination in the early years of the schools is notably lacking. This 'narrative of success and progress' was not unique to the Irish reformers.[119] It was decades before Murray's successor, John Lentaigne, told of his astonishment that Murray had brought leg bolts to restrain the girls in High Park. When Murray wrote of the 'complete success' of the regime in Limerick in 1867[120] he failed to mention the fact that two girls, Mary Delaney and Margaret Mills, had attempted to burn down the school.[121] He described a particular problem in the schools for girls – the difficulty of placing those who had been 'acquainted with vice' in employment. The class of girls who, he believed, could not be reformed were of the kind who would later be found in the punishment cells of convict prisons, whose 'sole satisfaction appears to be to shock even the most experienced prison officers ... with a language consisting of only ribaldry, blasphemy, and obscenity'.[122] He was of the opinion that '[i]n the Girls' Schools all the evil qualities of a woman's nature are rife'.[123]

In 1872 'several cases of violent hysterical and epileptic seizures' and 'acute mania' in High Park were reported. It was alleged that gangs of thieves taught girls to simulate epilepsy well enough to deceive the medical profession as a means of avoiding a reformatory sentence.[124] They may have been aware that the medical officer of a gaol had to sign a questionnaire which contained the question 'Is [the prisoner] scrofulous, or subject to fits?' to certify a child for fitness to be sent to a reformatory.[125] Eliza Rothe, superintendent of Grangegorman prison, told a government enquiry that, while in transit from court in the prison van, older prisoners told young girls to 'pretend that they had fits' so that they would not be kept in separation.[126] Whether the girls feigned the seizures or were suffering from an illness is not known but the inspector of lunatic asylums was brought to examine the girls, and more work in the outdoors and 'large and airy dormitories' were recommended.[127]

The challenge of dealing with 'very vicious and very artful girls' who had been transferred from High Park to Limerick was ably met by Mrs Lockwood, according to Murray. She 'cannot be deceived, and ... will not be cajoled', he wrote,[128] but it was not just the city girls who gave trouble. The inspector believed that country girls who had been criminal for some time were 'more devoid of good principles of conduct [and] more addicted to deceit ... [and] their passions [we]re more violent'. These girls were 'less impressionable, and more difficult of reformation'.[129] In 1867 he gave an account of a girl who was considered 'hopelessly irreclaimable' by the police, but who had obtained a position as a kitchen maid in a 'respectable' house after her release. Murray wrote that he could not 'speak too highly' of the training in the school.[130] Elsewhere, the challenge of reforming the Dublin girls seems to have been less successful. It would appear that by 1863 Mrs Kirwan, the manager of Goldenbridge, had had enough of Dublin's young female criminals. She closed the school in June and arranged for thirteen girls to be transferred to other schools, and for eight to be pardoned and sent to America, where she had organised employment for them. All eight were reported to be 'doing well'.[131]

The most consistently documented form of insubordination in the institutions was absconding, a phenomenon that continued in Irish reformatory and industrial schools into the twentieth century.[132] Escape, described by Stephen Toth as 'the most obvious indication of prisoner agency and resistance',[133] was recorded in the annual reports and occurred in every year. Genevieve Beale wrote of one girl, 'E.B', who twice absconded from Dublin reformatories, served six months' imprisonment as a result, and was eventually sent to Spark's Lake. 'E.B.' 'almost considered herself an outcast, cared for by none, and seemed quite reckless as to what she did …'[134] Sr Genevieve described two contrasting cases of other girls who escaped. 'A.M.' was a child with a 'roving and unsettled disposition' who would leave her 'comfortable' home to go thieving with persons of bad character. Her father had her prosecuted and asked the magistrates to commit her to a reformatory. She was sent to Spark's Lake but disappeared during prayers one spring morning. She was found eight or nine miles away and brought back, saying that she had gone looking for birds' nests and bluebells. 'Her large collection of wild flowers, and the grief she evinced when they were taken from her, proved the veracity of her statement'. 'T.' was the daughter of a poor widow who also met with bad company going to and from her job as a furniture polisher and 'was led through the different phases of vice'. She was committed to Spark's Lake to separate her from her former companions in Dublin. 'Forks, spoons, slates, snuffers, &c. became implements to effect the *one* end – her escape'. She was locked into a room but managed to remove some panelling and jump fourteen feet, and 'was in the act of scaling the garden wall when the rustling of the shrubs attracted attention'. She made three attempts to escape and was recaptured each time. Her eventual good behaviour was rewarded with a 'relaxation of discipline' and association with the other children in the daytime. By the spring of 1862, 'T' was on the list for promotion to the class of honour.[135]

Murray believed that absconding could be made advantageous if the child was recaptured because it made the staff more vigilant, convinced the public that the reformatories were 'not so attractive', and served as a cautionary lesson to other inmates.[136] Most of the children that escaped were recaptured and some, like the three Monaghan girls, surrendered themselves. A small number managed to remain at large, so that by 1871 there were eleven boys and three girls who had not been retaken.[137] These accounts of resistance demonstrate that the children detained in these institutions were not always passive recipients of the discipline imposed on them, but were, from time to time, active agents in defying the regimes in the reformatories.[138]

Expectations, outcomes and challenges

In 1869 when asked if he was happy with the working of the reformatory system in Ireland, Patrick Joseph Murray wrote that he was 'satisfied beyond my most sanguine expectations'. He explained the effect of juvenile crime, if unchecked, on society:

> In a thousand ways the vices of the poorer affect the richer classes. The children of our neglected homes spread the contagion of their vices abroad. The little Arab of the streets becomes a tempter in his turn. The outcast girl who is cast upon the *pavé* by the intemperance or neglect of her parents, becomes the seducer of our youth.[139]

By providing education and training for children who had been convicted of crime, Murray believed that they would become law-abiding and self-supporting citizens. For some children, the reformatories may have provided shelter, stability and training that would not have been accessible to them in the harsh world of post-Famine Ireland. The school managers reported on the 'disposal' of the children who left their schools. These reports were included in the annual reports of the government inspector. For both girls and boys, finding employment on their release from a reformatory was considered a priority, and one which could prove challenging for managers. Some managers favoured emigration for their former inmates, especially if it was thought that they would return to family or friends who were criminal or would exploit the children. In the early years of the Upton reformatory the school had arranged for boys to be sent to 'the New World of Brazil' on discharge,[140] and by 1870, ninety-five of the 257 inmates discharged in the previous nine years had emigrated. One had become a partner to a merchant in South America. One former Upton boy became a professor of mathematics and was 'in receipt of a handsome salary'.[141] Of the remainder, the manager reported that seven had died, fourteen had been reconvicted, and the remainder 'went to sea, enlisted, became servants, or returned to their friends'.[142]

In Spark's Lake, Murray wrote, some 'ill-disposed parents ... watch and wait' until the girls are about to be discharged in order to take them away 'for the purpose of living upon their gains by prostitution'.[143] In his annual report of 1867 he included an appendix in which Genevieve Beale gave an account of the lives of eighteen girls after they had left the school, including seven who had emigrated. One was 'C.T.' She had been sent to Spark's Lake after absconding from one of the Dublin schools. She arrived in Monaghan 'depraved and immoral, having had a very bad mother'. In order to avoid her return to such a mother, she was sent to America where she got a 'respectable' job in New Jersey. A fellow passenger on the voyage was so struck by her 'modest demeanour' that he proposed. She declined his offer because he was 'not religious'.[144] Julia Connolly, who had escaped from High Park and was brought back by her parents, was sent to Spark's Lake and was reported to be 'doing well' in America after her discharge. Margaret and Mary, who had attempted to burn the Limerick reformatory, were also sent to the Monaghan school. After her discharge, Margaret went to live with her father and cared for him into old age. Mary's 'subsequent career [was] very doubtful'.[145]

For some children, the strict regimes, deprivations and separation from family and friends were unendurable. Recent research has challenged the view that inmates of institutions like Mettray were 'automatons who mindlessly submit[ted] to their keepers'.[146] As previously alluded to, in the Irish reformatories many children resisted the discipline imposed on them by refractory behaviour and abscondings, and in some cases staff struggled to control them. Some refractory or absconding children found themselves again before the courts and returning to prison. For many former inmates, adjusting to life outside of the institutions must have been difficult, and some relapsed into crime.[147] In 1871 the reformatory managers reported that, of the 494 children discharged in the three prior years, 140 had been sent to 'employment or service', 141 had 'returned to friends' and twenty-seven had been convicted of crime.[148] It is probable that the real figure for the latter outcome was higher.

By 1870 the reformatories were facing significant financial challenges. While the Limerick girls brought in a profit from laundry work, the admirable needlework of the Monaghan girls had to be disposed of at a loss as there was no market for it.[149] By the end of its first decade Malone had new buildings and seventy-one inmates but the committee had incurred debt in its expansion, 'their appeal for aid not having been sufficiently met by the public'. Glencree recorded a loss of £108 in that year.[150] The problem many of the schools now faced was that Ireland was apparently seeing a dramatic decline in crime. Murray and others had cited the vastly increased criminal statistics of the post-Famine period in order to convince the government and public of the need for reformatories. In 1861 Richard Smyth questioned the 'hot haste' to pass the reformatory legislation at a time when crime in Ireland was 'hastening to extinction'.[151] When Murray began his campaign in 1854, there had been 10,786 committals of children to county and town gaols in Ireland. This represented nearly 18 per cent of all prisoners for that year. By the time the Davenport Hills visited the gaols and reformatories in 1865, they found that 'none of the Reformatories ... [we]re full; such [wa]s the decrease of juvenile crime in Ireland'.[152] In 1870 there were 1,313 committals of children to these gaols, with child criminals comprising 4 per cent of all committals. Managers of the schools were complaining to Murray

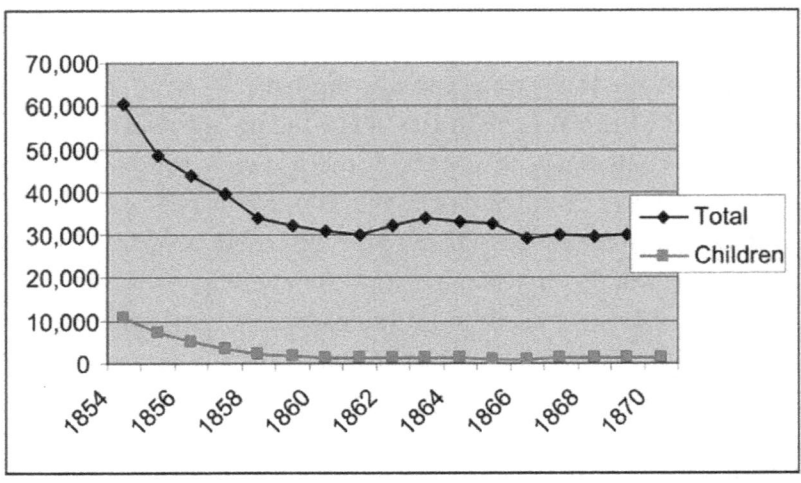

Table 2: Committals to prison, 1854 to 1870

that they could not be kept open without 'serious loss'.[153] The decline in numbers had already begun when Sergeant Deasy had brought the bill for the establishment of reformatories before parliament. The chief secretary had said that 'the evil which his honourable and learned Friend proposed to deal with was hardly of sufficient gravity to justify a special Act of Parliament'.[154] Despite such opposition, and undeterred by the statistics, Deasy and his supporters in parliament managed to not only push the legislation through but to shape it to their requirements.

John Lentaigne had taken over the job of inspector from Patrick Joseph Murray in 1870. In the mid-1860s Murray had been given the position of director of convict prisons and registrar of habitual criminals,[155] and his engagement with the system which he worked so hard to establish had begun to wane.[156] His successor brought long and varied experience in public administration to the post.[157] Lentaigne, who had a background in medicine, had been inspector-general of prisons since 1854 and had been appointed a commissioner of national education in 1861. He had also served as magistrate and high sheriff in Monaghan and had been on the committees for both the Spark's Lake and Glencree reformatories. Although he was nearly seventy when he took up the post of inspector of reformatories, he brought a rigour and vitality to the role that Murray lacked in his later years. He would need all of his energy. To the job of inspecting reformatories was now added the inspection of new institutions which would transform the way that poor children were treated in Ireland.

Chapter 3

'Unstained by Criminality'? Poor and criminal children, 1868–80

IN THE 1860s the focus of the reformers' attention turned to poor children. These children were regarded by some as pre-delinquent,[1] the 'well-spring' from which the future criminal population would emerge, and by others as vulnerable and in need of care. A campaign began in Ireland to introduce legislation for the establishment of industrial schools for such children. When it came, the legislation also made provision for very young criminal children to be sent to these schools. By 1868, there were three institutions for the incarceration of children convicted of crime in Ireland – industrial schools, reformatories and gaols.

Industrial schools

Although the two decades following the Famine had seen a significant reduction in the numbers of people entering Irish workhouses, there were still many children for whom they were home, either with or without their families. In a six-month period ending in September 1867, a total of 171,664 people were relieved in the workhouses. Of these, 52,073 were children aged under fifteen. Almost half of them were accompanied by their parents, 13,459 were orphaned or unaccompanied children, and a similar number were classed as illegitimate. The smallest classification of children in the workhouses at the time was the 112 described as '[l]unatics, insane persons, and idiots'.[2]

In 1861 Paul Cullen gave evidence to a government committee investigating the administration of poor relief in Ireland. He told the committee that many people considered the workhouse 'the most dangerous place that any poor man or poor boy can go to' and that 'with respect to the females the case is still worse'. He quoted an earlier investigation which stated that young girls were particularly vulnerable due to the influence of 'women of the town' and procuresses who tried to entice them to leave some workhouses to engage in prostitution. In the south Dublin workhouse there was a 'constant circulation from the workhouse to the streets, and to the brothels'.[3] Cullen was critical of the administration of the Poor Law system in Ireland and believed it should be reformed.[4] He was not alone in his criticism of the system and the manner in which it dealt with children. Many people now regarded the life of the workhouse child as the antithesis of 'the Victorian middle-class ideal of a happy childhood'.[5]

One year after the select committee of 1861 sat, legislation was passed extending to five the age at which a deserted or orphaned child could be boarded out to a foster family, and giving discretionary powers to guardians of workhouses to extend this to the age of eight if they felt it benefited the child's health.[6] Children living with families who were no longer receiving payment for them, however, frequently found themselves back in the workhouse. When a prison inspector found a girl of ten in the female prison at Grangegorman in 1869, he wrote that the system of returning children from families to the workhouse contributed to criminality: 'it is not wonderful that, shut up in the workhouse, young girls without a mother or female friend to advise, should sometimes ... find their way into the gaol'.[7]

In addition to the debates about workhouse children, there was also concern about the numbers of destitute and vagrant children who were still visible in public places. In the early 1860s one man decided to quantify the vagrant and criminal population which was 'at large' in Ireland. William Neilson Hancock was a mathematician, barrister, academic and founder of the Dublin Statistical Society.[8] The society had hosted the reading of papers by reformers regarding crime and the treatment of juvenile criminals since the early 1850s. In 1863 Neilson Hancock began to collect and collate information which he would subsequently present to parliament annually as judicial statistics. They provided a new range of data which included criminals, suspected criminals and vagrants. This information was collected by the police and included categories such as 'Known thieves and depredators', 'Receivers of stolen goods', 'Suspected persons' and 'Vagrants and tramps'.[9]

Neilson Hancock's first report included a table which compared these categories for Ireland with England and Wales. There were, according to the judicial statistics, 3,399 vagrants and tramps in Ireland under the age of sixteen in 1863, which Neilson Hancock estimated to be, in proportion to population, almost twice as many as in England and Wales. This contrasted significantly with the comparison of the 'criminal classes' in each jurisdiction, with an estimate of 370 child 'known thieves and depredators' in Ireland and a comparative figure of 1,135 in England and Wales. These categories of 'criminal classes' are generally challenged in modern discussions of criminality but in the 1860s they influenced public opinion and administration.[10] 'The number of youthful vagrants', Neilson Hancock wrote, 'are reduced in England and Wales by the operation of the Industrials Schools Acts'.[11] It was these vagrant children and those who were found in the company of criminals that the Irish reformers now focused their attention on.

The O'Conor Don, a Liberal Catholic MP for Roscommon, brought a private member's bill before parliament in 1867 which proposed the extension of the industrial school system to Ireland.[12] This system had been established in Britain since the 1850s. In bringing the bill before parliament, he had the full support of Paul Cullen, by now Ireland's first cardinal.[13] Some members of the Protestant, and particularly northern Presbyterian, community were opposed to the proposed legislation. They had witnessed the growing strength and confidence of the Catholic Church and feared that the government support recommended in the legislation would bolster the expansion of its institutions. It has been estimated that 3,500 children were in Catholic orphanages or foster homes in Dublin alone by 1864. Echoing the response of the Catholic bishops to the reformatory bills in the 1850s, Protestant MPs told parliament that it was 'a considerable infringement of personal liberty' to take up children for vagrancy and send them to a 'prison' for a long time.[14]

When the bill was brought before parliament for a second reading in March 1867, the O'Conor Don described the class of children that he proposed would be supported in industrial schools in Ireland:

... those wandering and begging in the streets – those without any protectors, without any visible means of obtaining a livelihood ... the miserable little wretches at present growing up in ignorance, idleness and crime.

When defending the bill against what Chichester Fortescue described in the House of Commons as 'the lamentable prejudice of many persons of the Presbyterian denomination in Ulster', the O'Conor Don outlined the benefits to society of such institutions. 'By taking up unfortunate vagrant children,' he told the house, 'and rearing them in the habits of industry you diminish the danger of having to support them afterwards as criminals'.[15] As further evidence of the need for industrial schools, he cited the judicial statistics for Ireland for the previous year. Like Neilson Hancock, the O'Conor Don attributed the comparatively low number of child vagrants in Britain outlined in the judicial statistics to the fact that industrial schools already existed in England and Wales. Despite his best efforts, the bill was unsuccessful. There were strong objections from northern Protestants. John Vance, MP for Armagh, said when the bill reached committee stage that 'monastic schools would be increased at the public expense'.[16] Lord Naas was not supportive, the process stalled, and was carried over to the next parliamentary session.

In 1868 the O'Conor Don was back before parliament with another industrial schools bill. This time it had the reluctant support of the chief secretary. It was successful and was enacted in May of that year. The Industrial

Schools Act of 1868 provided that any child under the age of fourteen years who was found begging, 'wandering and not having any Home or settled Place of Abode, or proper Guardianship or visible Means of Subsistence', a destitute orphan or a child whose parent or parents were in gaol, or who was frequenting the company of thieves, could be brought before a court by any person as a suitable case for the new industrial schools. Young criminal children were also provided for in the act. Section 13 stated that children under the age of twelve who were convicted of crimes which were not felonies could be sent to industrial schools where the justices or magistrates deemed it appropriate.

The funding model for the industrial schools was similar to that of the reformatories. The schools would be established under voluntary management and the Treasury would contribute to the maintenance of the children while in the schools.[17] The inspector of reformatories also became inspector of industrial schools. Although criminal children could be sent to the new industrial schools for misdemeanours, John Lentaigne saw a clear distinction between the types of children for whom the two types of school were established. Of the industrial school children, he wrote:

> These children are untainted by crime. The very fact of a conviction for a felonious offence renders a child ineligible for an Industrial School. There is no blot on them and they are entitled to all the advantages which the State provides in primary schools for the working classes.[18]

The response to the legislation initially disappointed its promoters. Only five schools had opened by 1869 and Patrick Joseph Murray described the legislation as a 'dead letter' in its first year.[19] In June of that year Mary Carpenter addressed a group of people that included the lord chancellor and the mayor of Dublin at the home of Walter Crofton in Merrion Square in Dublin in support of the system.[20] As more industrial schools began to open, the situation changed quickly. Children appeared at petty sessions, either alone or in groups, sometimes brought by the police for asking for alms, and sometimes brought by clergy or members of the public. One of the first industrial schools to open was a school for boys in Salthill in Galway which had a capacity for 100 children. John Lentaigne wrote that '[t]he people of Galway ... have shown a public spirit and anxiety to benefit the wretched little boys found wandering through the district'.[21] Newspaper reports of the Galway courts reveal how this 'public spirit' was translated into action. On 20 November 1872, six 'destitute' boys were ordered by a Galway petty sessions court to be sent to the new school. A week later, the same court saw three such cases brought before it. The first, 'Head Constable Shore v. John Summerly 10 years old', resulted in John being sent to the Salthill industrial school for six years. The second case, 'William Wylde v. Thomas Higgins aged 11 years', led to a detention order of five years for Thomas. The third, 'The Police v. Denis Fahy, Nicholas Flemming, John Burns, James Flynn, John McDonagh, William Regan, John Wynn, Patrick Carmody', resulted from the arrest of the boys 'for soliciting alms in the streets'. They were all sent to the Salthill school. By January 1873, the school was full.[22] By the end of 1873, fifty-two industrial schools had opened and had 4,360 children detained in them.[23]

Within five years of the legislation, the industrial schools had four times as many children in them as the reformatories. Such was the surge in detention orders that Dublin Castle wrote to magistrates in January 1873 reminding them of the classes of children who were fit subjects for the schools.[24] Jane O'Brien has written that 'industrial school places were hard to come by in the early decades of the system',[25] and Jane Barnes has also outlined how demand for places in the schools put pressure on the system, noting that children were left in workhouses indefinitely while waiting to be admitted to industrial schools.[26]

One class of children that was not filling the new schools were those who had been convicted of a crime. In 1870 twenty-five children under the age of ten, and sixty-seven aged between ten and twelve, were sent to reformatories. Maria Kean, who was eight years old, just a year above the age of criminal responsibility, was given a five-year reformatory sentence in Galway in 1872 for the crime of larceny.[27] There were, at the time, five industrial schools for girls in the county. In January 1875 six-year-old Thomas Healy and seven-year-old Henry Bishop broke into a house in Nicholas Street in Dublin and stole a pair of trousers and a vest which they pawned for six shillings. When asked what they had spent the money on, they replied to the court that they had bought cakes, sweets and squibs (small fireworks). The boys' youth did not move the magistrate, who sentenced them to five years each in Philipstown reformatory, telling them that he was saving them from leading a life of crime.[28] In his first report as inspector, John Lentaigne wrote: 'I regret to observe so large a number of young children are still sent to Reformatory Schools, some so young as scarcely to be accountable for criminal acts'. He laid the blame at the feet of the magistrates and, while admitting that 'there was a tendency in Ireland not to convict young offenders of first offences', reminded them of the provision for such children in the Industrial Schools Act.[29] In Nenagh petty sessions in October 1873, a dispute arose on the bench as to how to deal with 'a very small boy', Michael Hannon, who had brought a stolen sheet to a pawnbroker, who, in turn, sent for the police. The chair of the bench, Caleb Going, had enquired into the boy's character, and found it good, and believed that he was too young to be sent to a reformatory. He was overruled and Michael was given a five-year reformatory sentence.[30] In May 1874 a circular was sent to magistrates again reminding them of the provisions of the industrial schools legislation, including section 13.[31]

As the industrial school system evolved, the reluctance of the managers to accept children who had been convicted of misdemeanours into their institutions meant that these children were essentially locked out of the schools. By 1880, when there were 150 boys aged between seven and eleven who had been committed to the three Catholic boys' reformatories in Glencree, Upton and Philipstown,

Lentaigne had received so many complaints from magistrates about the refusal of industrial school managers to receive young children that he was forced to take action. The managers complained that accepting criminal children cast a 'stigma' on their schools and the children in them. Jane Barnes has written that some industrial school managers were reluctant to allow their children to mix with others living in their area 'lest the carefully-tended industrial children should suffer from communication with free children'.[32] Lentaigne and others were more concerned about the 'deplorable results' that fourteen days in gaol in the company of adult prisoners, and the subsequent years spent in a reformatory, would have on young offenders. 'Who would dream', he wrote, 'of placing a child suffering from a trifling ailment in the wards of an hospital with patients undergoing treatment for contagious diseases'. The solution, for boys only, was to open a 'probationary' industrial school in Kilmore, near the Artane industrial school, in County Dublin. The school would be run by the Christian Brothers and would only accept criminal boys under twelve. Once they reached the age of twelve, they could be transferred to another industrial school or returned to family.[33]

Not only were the industrial school managers refusing to accept young criminal children into their schools, they were also prosecuting refractory children in their care in order to have them sent to gaols or reformatory schools. In the eleven years from 1870 to 1880, ninety-five children – fifty-six boys and thirty-nine girls – were brought to court by industrial school managers and sent to reformatories.

The majority, sixty-six children, were prosecuted for running away from the schools. In one year, 1877, eight boys were sent to reformatories for absconding from the Artane school alone. Jane Barnes recounts the story of one boy, Daniel Conway, who escaped from the school four times before being sentenced to five years in Philipstown.[34] The sixty-six only represent those who were caught and sent to a reformatory, so the real figure for absconding from industrial schools is likely to have been higher. The threat of arrest, court, gaol and then a long sentence in a reformatory must have acted as a powerful disincentive to the children from running away, and therefore it is probable that most of the children did not do so lightly.[35] Not all attempts by managers to have children removed from their schools were successful. When, in January 1873, a Galway priest brought some boys to court for fighting in his industrial school, the magistrate refused to send them to a reformatory because 'the fact of one boy striking another is rather poor grounds for having him sent among criminals for 4 or 5 years'. The magistrate ordered that the boys be returned to the industrial school with a caution.[36]

By 1884, there were sixty-four industrial schools in Ireland with 6,296 children detained in them.[37] This was almost twice the number of homeless children which the judicial statistics had estimated were in Ireland two decades earlier. It was suggested that poor but respectable parents with large families were choosing one child and sending that child out to beg to have them sent to an industrial school.[38] There would appear to have been greater public support for the new schools than for the reformatories, perhaps because the public were more sympathetic to children who were victims of poverty than those who were perpetrators of crime. Official attitudes to the industrial school child also differed, despite claims by supporters of reformatories that criminal children were deserving of sympathy and less harsh treatment than adult offenders. In the words of the commissioner of national education, industrial school children were believed to be:

> Unstained by criminality ... a thoroughly innocent and religious class, and, as the victims of poverty or neglect, most interesting objects of sympathy and charity.[39]

Reformatories

As the industrial school system went through a rapid expansion, reformatories were reaching their zenith in terms of numbers of institutions and inmates. John Lentaigne brought a more rigorous style to the job of inspector than his predecessor, Murray. He sometimes found himself in conflict with the managers of both industrial and reformatory schools. The manager of Artane industrial school described his method of inspection as follows:

> Sir John Lentaigne, who comes to us morning and evening, and at all hours, would not wait to knock at the door, but he goes into every part of the place, and goes through the schools and looks at the classes and sees everything.[40]

In his first report he declared himself 'thoroughly informed of the condition and treatment of the pauper and criminal classes of the juvenile population in Ireland' because of his vast experience as a magistrate, a Poor Law guardian, inspector of prisons and commissioner of national education.[41]

By December 1870 there were 995 children in reformatories. The majority, 810, were boys. In 1870 the managers of Glencree had leased premises in Philipstown, King's County, and St Conleth's reformatory was certified at this site. The buildings were formerly a cavalry barracks and a convict depot, had a high wall around them, and were surrounded by bog. Lentaigne thought the reformatory promised to be one of the best in Ireland. Within five years of opening, Philipstown held 369 boys.[42] The Oblates had borrowed heavily to extend and renovate the buildings in both their schools and to buy adjacent land. Such was the level of debt incurred that the committee that had founded Glencree, which included Lord Fitzgerald, Lord O'Hagan and Lentaigne, resigned. By the early 1880s, none of the Catholic schools had committees. John Lentaigne later told a government enquiry that he had seen money spent on 'useless buildings'.[43]

The facilities at Philipstown impressed him, however. A lavatory, with 'separate basin, towel, comb and brush for each boy', had been completed. Farm buildings and 'trade shops' had also been built. Boys were trained as carpenters, smiths, harness-makers, coopers, painters, shoemakers, tailors, bakers and stonecutters, and in the manufacture of gas for the school. Most of the boys, as in Glencree, were engaged in agricultural labour and in the reclamation of the boggy land which surrounded the school. In severe weather, also as in Glencree, younger boys were put knitting and sewing. A schoolteacher who had qualified under the national education system was employed to teach the boys for three-and-a-half hours a day. Brass and string bands were formed and were considered to be beneficial.

Despite these successes, other aspects of the school gave strong indications that all was not well. From Lentaigne's earliest reports, it is obvious that there were problems with the health and discipline of the boys, yet it is remarkable that Lentaigne was not more critical of the management of the school. In all but two years between 1872 and 1880, a number of boys died in Philipstown. The managers defended their position by saying that the boys came to them in an unhealthy state, citing one example of a boy who had for years slept in a cavity in the wall of a railway bridge before his admission, and had subsequently died in the school.[44] The deaths of eighteen boys in this period, including one by suicide, should have been more of a cause for concern for the inspector, particularly as Lentaigne's medical background lent a 'quasi-medical' aspect to his inspections.[45] There was no proper heating in the buildings, and cases of pneumonia were frequent. This was another shortcoming of the institution that Lentaigne overlooked; he merely commented rather passively in 1881 that 'no attempt has been made to put up a heating apparatus ... it is hoped that it ... will be erected'.[46]

Figure 3: Tailor shop, Philipstown reformatory

Disciplinary problems also emerged in the school soon after its opening. In its first full year as a reformatory, 'a few bad spirits' gave trouble. When the inspector of prisons visited the King's County gaol in 1873, he found a young man serving a one-year sentence for having violently assaulted the manager of Philipstown with a knife.[47] Children absconded from the school and a reward was offered to anyone who 'captured' an escapee. Lentaigne suggested that the old prison, which had been used for convicts, be used to lock up the absconders, and that they wear a different uniform and be placed in a 'class of dishonour', describing it as a 'Penal Reformatory for boys'.[48] The boys were locked into cells at night and a watchman patrolled the building. This solitary confinement was 'much dreaded' by the boys.[49] It did not deter them, however. In 1878 eighteen boys absconded. Most were retaken within a short time with the assistance of the local people.[50]

Lentaigne was much more critical of Philipstown's sister school, Glencree. While the second school was opened to alleviate the crowded conditions in the Wicklow reformatory, the inspector repeatedly complained of conditions in Glencree in his annual reports. The health of the boys was also a concern. Smallpox and typhoid were responsible for the deaths of boys and a staff member in the 1870s. While acknowledging the manager's claims that a boy brought smallpox into the school with him after a visit to Dublin 'where small-pox then raged', and praising the measures taken by the brothers to contain the epidemic which affected over sixty boys, Lentaigne blamed conditions at the school for the way in which it took hold:

> Disease does not attack an institution to the extent to which this school has suffered, unless there are powerful exciting causes to superinduce it ... defective sanitary arrangements in this instance may have predisposed the inmates to the infection.[51]

It is also likely that hard, physical work on a mountainside would have contributed to the boys' ill health. Most of the boys were still reclaiming the 120 acres of wild land on which the school was situated. In October 1874 four boys died when a bank of land under which they were working fell on them.[52] The lack of indoor facilities was a source of great exasperation for Lentaigne. In 1878 he complained that 'year after year' he had urged the managers to erect a hall where the boys could exercise when it snowed or rained.[53] The absence of adequate heating would also have contributed to illness. It was only in 1880, twenty-one years after its foundation, that Glencree had a heating system installed, and then only in the chapel. In his annual report the inspector expressed the wish that another year would not go by without all of the problems being addressed:

> It is hoped that the heating apparatus can also be utilised for the dormitories and school-rooms, which, in the cold climate of Glencree, on the Wicklow mountains, at a height of 1,800 feet above the sea would be most desirable. Neither has the play-hall or the additional workshops and appliances, the proposed infirmary, and other buildings, which are so much required, been erected.[54]

The literary education of the boys was somewhat better with reading, writing, arithmetic, spelling and geography being taught, although Lentaigne complained of the lack of trained teachers. In the early 1870s the Oblates made a basic level of literacy a condition of releasing boys on licence before the expiration of their sentences. For some, this would appear to have been an unattainable goal. The parents of William Barry, who had been sent to Glencree in June 1869, petitioned to have him released early three years into his sentence. In her petition his mother wrote that the schoolmaster had written to her saying that he was 'well inclined' and improving. She claimed that:

> The Revd Father Fox told him not to take to the band for if he did he could not get home at half his time. It seems so strange that other boys have got home before their time quite as ignorant. My son was delicate from his birth and I am told by boys that have been liberated that he cannot eat the stirabout.

The reply from Glencree was that they would 'keep him up to the last day of his term' if he did not improve at school. They cited the case of another boy who had only been released 'by order'. 'Only for that', they wrote, he too would have been kept to the last day of his sentence, 'for he was quite as ignorant, and even more stupid than William Barry is'. If the Barry family's claims are true, the managers of Glencree were selecting the more skilled boys, like those in the band, for retention, and not offering them early release on licence which was their right under the legislation. Their petition was rejected.[55] In 1874 Glencree eventually hired a certified and trained teacher, under pressure from Lentaigne. It came too late for William Barry, who might have benefited from such training, as this was the same year that his sentence expired.

Discipline was also a recurring problem for Glencree. In 1872 the inspector wrote that '[f]rom no other school in Ireland have so many boys absconded as from this'. He blamed the lack of 'the element of hope' for the boys in the school, and, in particular, the refusal of the managers to release boys early on licence.⁵⁶ While the managers reported that the majority of boys were well conducted, the escapes continued. In 1878 photography was introduced as a trade in the school and pictures of the boys were taken so that the escapees could be identified.⁵⁷ The fact that boys were willing to navigate the hard mountain terrain, with the risk of being caught and punished, either in gaol or within the 'iron prison' in Philipstown or the punishment cells of Glencree, should have alerted Dublin Castle to the problems within the two reformatories.

Descriptions of children who absconded were advertised in the police gazette, *Hue and Cry*. A boy who gave his name to the police as Patrick Stevens joined in the laughter of the court when his description – 'cock nose, and large mouth' – was read out. He had been arrested while sleeping in a doorway in Cork by a policeman who recognised him from his description and from his clothes, which had a piece cut out of the jacket 'where the number should appear'. Patrick, who had a strong Dublin accent, told the court that he had walked to Cork 'to see the big city' and go to the races. He initially denied that he had been in a reformatory and told the court that he would 'go back to the big smoke – Guinness's smoke'. As he was about to be remanded, he asked to address the magistrates and admitted to them that he had entered Glencree at 'the time of the Fenians, the time of the big snow when I found a whole lot of pikes. I am a Fenian, and I'll die a Fenian too'.⁵⁸

In one week in January 1872 six boys appeared in court in Kingstown and Dublin charged with absconding from

Glencree. It was the second time that one of them had escaped.[59] Patrick Nolan, who was about eleven years old, appeared at Nenagh petty sessions in 1874, accused of having escaped from the school. He had previously been acquitted of the charge of highway robbery. Glencree sent one of its employees, William Costigan, to bring Patrick back. In court, Patrick 'shoved himself against' Costigan, asked him 'what the d[evi]l brought him there' and claimed that other boys in the reformatory had kicked and beaten him. Patrick was sent to Nenagh gaol for a month, with hard labour, and was then to be returned to Glencree to finish out his sentence. He was warned by the chair of the bench that if he escaped again he would be given a six-month sentence, with that sentence 'repeated again and again, should [he] succeed in escaping out of the place'.[60] Perhaps the most spectacular of all escapes occurred from Malone reformatory in 1875 when thirty-seven boys, half of the school population, escaped in one night in May. All but three were retaken and the ringleaders were sent to gaol.[61]

The worst indictment of the reformatory system was that children who had been in the schools would reoffend. While a small number of recidivists could be expected, the number of reoffenders who had been in Glencree and Philipstown was high and did not escape the attention of those outside the system, in particular some members of the bench. In 1877 a Dublin magistrate before whom two young men appeared charged with multiple burglaries remarked that 'it was a curious coincidence that both defendants had undergone five years each in the Philipstown reformatory, educated together'.[62] In an address to the Statistical and Social Inquiry Society in 1882 the recorder of Dublin described the criminal careers of two ex-reformatory boys who had appeared before him. Both had been to Glencree, and one had served five years there and five in Philipstown.[63] In 1879 the Catholic chaplain in Spike Island prison wrote that ex-reformatory boys were amongst the most troublesome and difficult to reform.[64] In the three years from 1873 to 1875, it was estimated that forty-one Glencree boys out of 310 were reconvicted of crime after discharge, although the real figure is likely to be higher.[65]

John Kelly served a five-year sentence in Glencree and was frequently sentenced to prison after his discharge. One of the difficulties that discharged reformatory inmates like John faced was re-entry into society. Five years of separation from family and friends would often have meant a severing of such ties, which left the boys without homes and support. They would also have faced great difficulty in finding work. While serving a sentence in Mountjoy, John asked permission of the governor to have access to a book on carpentry.[66]

An agent was appointed in Dublin to look after the welfare of discharged boys, but his duties changed in 1877 and he no longer looked after the former inmates.[67] Without homes or paid employment, for many the only alternative was to steal. This was not just a problem for the Glencree and Philipstown boys. At least thirty-four of 135 Upton inmates released between 1877 and 1879 were reconvicted of crime.[68] John Lentaigne wrote that discharged boys congregated together in the large towns like Cork, and one bad boy could 'do much mischief'. On his visit to Upton in 1882, he found very young boys who, he said, should have been in a probationary institution like Kilmore. 'These boys', he wrote, 'when they leave the Institution, are just of an age to be influenced by evil minded persons who may have been their companions in the Reformatory'.[69]

It is also probable that the mental health of some children would have suffered during and after their sentences and that this would have affected their ability to cope with life outside the reformatories.[70] Being taken away from family and friends would have been traumatic for many children, and some newspaper accounts of their trials provide a glimpse of the reactions of the children and their families to their reformatory sentences. On the same day that Fr Fox placed a notice in the newspaper to inform magistrates that Philipstown was open to receive children, four boys cried and begged Dublin magistrate C.J. O'Donel to have mercy on them when he sentenced them to five years in the new reformatory for taking 'clothes of small value' from gardens in Rathgar. Matthew McGarry 'became violent and roared and cried' and had to be brought to the cells of a Dublin court by two policemen 'in whose arms he continued to struggle' when he was given a five-year sentence to Glencree in 1879.[71] A young boy named Mahony burst into tears and screamed when told of his reformatory sentence. His mother told him to have courage, and that his father, who was in America, would send for him.[72] The father of a young Kerry boy was 'very much affected' when his child was about to be sentenced to a reformatory and successfully pleaded with the magistrates to have the sentence reduced.[73] The mother of William Webbe, 'an intelligent, good-looking boy', was not so successful. William was found in possession of a stolen lump of coal in Athy in 1876 and was given a three-year reformatory sentence. The local newspaper described the 'painful scene' that followed – 'Prisoner's mother clasped him convulsively in her arms, and both had to be removed from the court sobbing violently'.[74]

The harsh punishments inflicted on children in the reformatories would also have taken their toll. The locking of children into punishment cells,[75] a common feature of the disciplinary regimes in all of the schools, was likely to have had a powerful effect on them, and evidence of the effects of long periods of separation on the mental health of adult prisoners in Britain had contributed to its decline in popularity.[76] Thomas Clarke described the 'maddening silence, sitting hopeless, friendless, and alone' of his time in Millbank prison.[77] It is not surprising, therefore, that the old 'iron prison' in Philipstown was 'much dreaded' by the boys. William McAvina from Leitrim served a five-year sentence there from 1873 to 1878. On his release, he returned to his family but was arrested within a short while for burglary. His parents thought his mind was 'not quite right'. He was taken to Carrick-on-Shannon gaol where he tried to hang himself. From there he entered the adult prison system in Mountjoy and Spike Island. While the medical officer in Mountjoy declared him to be of

Figure 4: William McAvina at the beginning and end of his prison sentence

sound mind, his time in prison was very disturbed and he was frequently punished. On his release from prison in 1885, he went to Liverpool.[78]

The lack of patronage societies to look after the welfare of discharged boys concerned Lentaigne and was a matter he felt many of the boys' schools neglected. Upton eventually employed a former head constable to visit discharged boys in Cork and give them advice, money, food and clothes when necessary. In 1880 John Lentaigne reported that the Oblates had been granted a certificate for Philipstown on condition that they establish a 'joint system of supervision' over boys who were either on licence or discharged from Glencree and the new reformatory. They did not do this, and he wrote that 'magistrates and judges with good reason complain of the results consequent on the neglect'.[79] The large numbers in the three Catholic boys' schools made such supervision difficult. By 1880, Glencree was still the biggest of all the Irish reformatories, with an average daily number of inmates of 276. Its sister school, Philipstown, was the second biggest with 274, and the third Catholic school for boys, Upton, had the third highest number at 245. It remained the case that only one reformatory in England had more inmates than each of these three Irish schools, the Philanthropic Society's school at Redhill in Surrey.[80] The Protestant boys' schools had much smaller numbers with an average of eighty-three in Malone and twenty-seven in Rehoboth.[81] While the large numbers of Catholic boys reflect the proportion of Catholic children who were imprisoned at the time,[82] the development of these large institutions over a relatively short period of time is remarkable.

The girls' schools rarely reached the capacity for which they were intended. High Park and Spark's Lake had the highest numbers of inmates, usually between forty and seventy in each. A new manager was appointed to High Park, and a costly programme of expansion included new buildings.[83] More trades were taught, including the making of fine gloves, and the literary education was improved. In 1881 Lentaigne described High Park as a 'model of order and cleanliness', where outdoor work had improved the girls both morally and physically. They were 'industrious, cheery and happy'. The discipline was 'firm but kind', and although some girls misbehaved and some were reconvicted after discharge, the manager, Mary Tobin, reported that she had so many requests for 'servants and trades workers' from members of the public that she was unable to supply them from her inmates.[84]

Girls whose behaviour could not be controlled in High Park were almost all sent to Spark's Lake in Monaghan, the 'penal reformatory school' for girls. Throughout her time as manager, Genevieve Beale maintained a policy of accepting girls that other schools would not take or could not cope with. Separation of new from older inmates and of hardened offenders from the more innocent was a cornerstone of the disciplinary regime of the school. Two inmates, Mary Fleming and her friend Mary Smith, were sent to Spark's Lake in 1871, having been convicted of stealing a coat from an establishment in Meath Street in Dublin. Mary wrote to her parents about not only being separated from them, but of separation within the institution as well:

Dear Mother and Father I am not with Mary Smith a tall I did not speake one word to her since I left Dublin we are in the one convent but not in the on school ... Dear father I am breaking my hart hear becaus I am so far away from yous all if I was a littel girl it would not be so bad but a big girl like me benigin my 5 years but dont fret maby it is all for the best.[85]

> Dear father I am breaking my
> hart hear Because I am so far
> away from yous all if I was
> a little girl it would not be
> so bad But a big girl Like me
> Bein[g] in my 5 years But dont
> fret maby it is all for the Best
> Dear mother Let me know did
> you get a [A]unces from my
> uncel James. yet Dear mother
> Let me know Would there Be
> any guee in ?itting to him
> to ask him to pay my paca[ge]
> to America for if I have to stay
> heare my hart will Breake
> Dear Father and mother tell mister
> Kelly not to for get the night
> me and margret Dog[e]rat[t]y drank
> the gallen of milk and woul[d]
> not give misses Kelly an[y] of

Figure 5: Letter from Mary Fleming, Spark's Lake reformatory

Lentaigne was impressed with the treatment and progress of the girls in Spark's Lake. One of the keys to the success of the school, he believed, was that, unlike in

Glencree, a sense of hope was fostered in the girls, and that they were told at the beginning of their sentence there that their pasts were forgotten and they would only be judged on their behaviour while in the school.[86] One girl, Beale reported to him, pretended to be insane for two months after admission, but was kept 'under constant supervision day and night by the Sisters and a few trustworthy girls' and at last 'gave in'.[87] The moral and physical well-being of the girls was, he believed, improved with outdoor work and a healthy diet which included cod liver oil, quinine and eggs. Lentaigne was also pleased with the standard of literary and vocational education which the girls were getting. Their schooling was better than in most other reformatories, and the girls were educated to the same standard as in the national schools. By 1876, the school had seventy-one inmates and they were engaged in fine and plain needlework, laundry work, dairying, cooking and in the making of mattresses. The school was making an 'industrial profit' of £152.[88]

In 1877 Genevieve Beale, the most formidable of all the reformatory managers, died. It was nineteen years since she had left France 'determined to devote her life to the reformation of unfortunate Irish girls'. While some managers of the new institutions were selective about the children they accepted, she appeared to relish the challenge of taking on and reforming girls considered by others to be incorrigible. She was also more successful at maintaining contact with discharged inmates than were most other managers. This maintenance of contact by the school continued after her death. In 1878 John Lentaigne expressed his satisfaction that, of the thirty-nine girls discharged in the previous three years, none had been lost sight of, 'showing how carefully the lady superintendent looks to the future of the girls confided to her care'. Three of the thirty-nine had been reconvicted of crime.[89]

In the early 1870s John Lentaigne's main concern regarding the girls' reformatory at Limerick was that the inmates were not kept sufficiently separate from the women in the Magdalene asylum, which the nuns also managed on the same site. He was critical of the standard of the literary education of the girls too – their answers to his questions on geography were 'loose and inaccurate' and arithmetic was neglected in the school. The industrial training was more productive. The girls learned needlework and household work, but, most significantly, they were bringing in 'considerable' profit from taking in laundry. This, he believed, was evidence that the girls were trained to be hard-working.[90]

When a new manager took over the running of the school in 1871, the schooling of the girls improved, but the industrial profit was reduced from £307 to £192.[91] The new manager would have to find a balance between providing education and training for the girls, while at the same time finding money for new buildings and running an institution which was largely dependent on Treasury funding. Managers of reformatories in Ireland had to source the money for buildings 'out of their private funds', whereas in England they could avail of money from rates.[92] In 1873 the forty-two inmates were removed to a new building on the lawn of the convent, separated from the Magdalene asylum.[93] In 1879 a site was purchased on which to build a much-needed new school. As well as continuing to bring in a profit from laundry, the girls were making Limerick lace. They were 'obedient, docile, very industrious and easily managed'. They were also, Lentaigne wrote, kindly treated.[94] By 1880, the nuns were caring for a consumptive girl whose time for discharge had passed but who had 'no friends'. Seven girls had left and gone to Australia and New Zealand. They had brought their lace patterns with them 'to be usefully employed on the voyage'. Two had married 'respectably' and wrote letters of gratitude to the nuns.[95]

The only Protestant reformatory for girls in Ireland, at Cork Street in Dublin, was also the smallest of all the schools. When in 1874 a 'spirit of insubordination' broke out in the school, some girls 'rallied round' the manager, Miss Cooke, a former prison officer, and helped to quell the bad behaviour.[96] In 1878 fourteen-year-old Mary Taylor appeared in court in Belfast a week after she absconded from the school. She told the court that she ran away because she was punished for being idle.[97] Such was the perceived success of Miss Cooke's regime that when a girl was transferred from an industrial school to Cork Street as incorrigible, her behaviour after a time became 'exemplary', and she was licensed out to employment with an 'excellent character'.[98] By 1880 the inspector claimed that an 'excellent spirit' prevailed amongst the eighteen inmates of the school.[99]

The reformatory school that was most consistently praised by John Lentaigne throughout the 1870s was the girls' school at Ballinasloe. The success of Ballinasloe was attributed by Lentaigne to a management style that he had referred to in other schools – the constant supervision, day and night, of the girls by the nuns.[100] In 1872 he described it as one of the best girls' reformatories in the kingdom. He portrayed the girls as 'robust and healthy', spending their days at laundry and needlework, household and farm work and at school.[101] By 1877, the nuns had imported bees from Italy, and the girls were harvesting honey.[102] In the early 1870s the school was undersubscribed, but the numbers were boosted by the admission of children considered troublesome in industrial schools. For girls in Ballinasloe for whom the ribbons did not have the desired disciplinary effect, 'cellular confinement' was used.[103] Only one girl was reported to have absconded from the school, and, of all the discharges in the 1870s, only two were reconvicted. 'Nowhere', Lentaigne wrote, 'is the reformation of young offenders more effectually carried out than in this school'.[104] The girls, he said, were made to feel that they were in a home where 'a holy spot in the heart of every child whose brain is not perverted by hereditary tendencies or disease' was reached.[105] By 1883, the school had only twenty-four inmates, even though it was capable of taking sixty.

For some children, the schools may have provided a refuge from a harsher world outside and may have given them opportunities they might not otherwise have had. A boy named Horgan told a Cork court that he wanted to pursue the trade of shoemaking that he had learned in Upton, but that his violent and alcoholic parents forced him to work 'morning, noon and night at boat-building' to pay for their alcohol.[106] The manager of Artane observed that all of the boys who came to the Kilmore school had been 'treated violently' before they arrived.[107] Twelve-year-old Patrick Devereux told the policeman who arrested him – for being found in the Gresham Hotel coffee room in possession of spoons and a knife – that he wanted to go to school. Magistrate O'Donel granted him his wish and sent him to Glencree.[108]

Many children were prosecuted by their parents, who used the courts to try to have them sent to reformatories. Fourteen-year-old Mary Matthews was accused by her mother of assaulting her and using profane and obscene language. Mary's mother claimed that the assault happened when she found her in the street in the company of soldiers, having been missing from home for some days. When magistrate O'Donel handed down a sentence of five years in a reformatory, Mary told him, 'Well, your worship, I will do just the same when I come out'.[109] Mary Rourke's 'respectable-looking' father charged her with stealing five shillings. Mary, along with some of her father's possessions, had also been missing from home, and her father feared that she had fallen in with bad company.[110]

By 1880, the number of children in reformatories had peaked at 1,160. The managers of the boys' schools claimed that, of the 618 boys released in the three years ending in 1880, 84 per cent were 'doing well', while 86 per cent of the 144 discharged girls were also stated to have been 'reformed'.[111] John Lentaigne wrote that:

> The responsibility of the managers of [reformatory and industrial] schools is indeed heavy ... the young persons whom they train must be brought up in health and honesty, with a knowledge of skilled labour fully equal to any in the market, so that they can support themselves in afterlife by their own industry.

This responsibility extended beyond their discharge. By the end of the 1870s managers reported that three times as many boys as girls were re-convicted of crime after their release from reformatories, something which Lentaigne attributed to 'a most careful supervision' of the conduct of the girls.[112]

Gaols

By 1868 two new types of institution existed in Ireland for the incarceration of criminal children – reformatories and industrial schools for the very young who had been convicted of non-felonious crime. Despite this, however, most children who were sentenced by the courts served out their sentences in the county and town gaols. In 1870 there were 1,313 committals of children to local gaols, of which 268 were given reformatory sentences, having first served the required fourteen days in gaol. By the end of the decade there were 986 committals to the gaols, of which 263 were sentenced to reformatory school.[113]

For most of the children who were sent to gaol at this time, their stay was a short one and was spent in one of the local gaols in their county or town. Of the 1,313 committals of children to these institutions in 1870, for example, 921, or 70 per cent, were for sentences of between twenty-four hours and one month. Similarly, five years later it was 72 per cent.[114] Conditions in these gaols varied and the children could find themselves in a large city gaol with hundreds of adult prisoners or in a small rural one with twenty or thirty other prisoners. The local gaols were subject to increasingly strict regulation and were rigorously inspected. Each had a board of superintendence which met every month or so, a government inspector who visited at least once a year, a local inspector who visited regularly, chaplains for each of the religions of the prisoners, and a medical officer. Their visits were recorded in the annual reports of the inspectors.

There were two government inspectors in the early 1870s,[115] one of whom was John Lentaigne. They questioned the prisoners on their diet and conditions and frequently took on board prisoners' complaints. The local inspectors usually visited at least once a week and sometimes more often. The chaplains also visited regularly and the medical officer attended sick prisoners. In Mayo county gaol in 1870, for example, the local inspector, chaplains, medical officer and an apothecary made 1,016 visits, while in Richmond bridewell these officers made 1,228 visits in the same year.[116] Any punishments meted out in the gaol were entered into a punishment book which was presented to the board of superintendence at its meetings for discussion.

While the rigour and quality of the inspections depended on the calibre of the various inspectors, they sometimes took an interest in individual prisoners and from time to time acted on their behalf. In 1869 in his report on Galway gaol the inspector noted from the punishment books that an eight-year-old prisoner was sentenced to twelve lashes, a punishment which he thought 'very severe for so young a child'. He found a nine-year-old girl, whose mother was in gaol and her father a 'travelling pedlar', serving a sentence for larceny from the person. 'The poor child', he noted, 'had sore eyes from hardship and bad food'. Her only hope, he wrote, was to be sent to a reformatory or industrial school. He also reported that the local inspector had 'taken charge' of another girl who had been in the gaol for stealing a pair of boots and had found her a job. When the government inspector visited Sligo gaol in August 1869, he met a young boy there who, he wrote, 'appeared to feel his position here extremely', leading him to believe that a 'misapprehension might have occurred in his case'. The inspector did not reveal whether he had investigated this possible miscarriage of justice any further.[117]

Richmond bridewell continued to be the busiest gaol in Ireland. In 1851 there had been almost 3,000 committals of children aged under fifteen to the large Dublin gaol.[118] By 1870, over 400 of the 4,176 committals were of boys aged sixteen and under, a proportion that was higher than in other gaols at the time and they accounted for approximately one-third of all committals of children in the country that year. When the inspector visited on 19 December 1870, he found eleven boys in custody, five of whom were serving their fourteen-day preliminary sentences before being sent on to a reformatory.[119] These boys were kept in separation, whereas the other boys, who were not being sent to a reformatory, mixed with adult prisoners at work or school during the day. The inspectors were anxious that this be changed. In 1871 a very young boy who had been convicted of stealing a mat was sent to Richmond for a week. The inspector spoke to the boy, who 'could hardly speak distinctly' and claimed to be nine years old. He believed that he was much younger. In his report, he wrote that such children should be sent to an industrial school, as he feared the effect that prison would have on 'such tender minds'. He noted that the Dublin magistrates should take more care in ascertaining the age of young criminals as they often lied about their ages in order to avoid a reformatory sentence which was considerably longer.[120]

Well-behaved prisoners under the age of twenty-five could attend school. The Richmond teacher had been trained in the Model School in Dublin and the Board of National Education carried out inspections. Schooling was for two hours a day and carried out in a room which had forty compartments in which the prisoners sat, separated from each other. On the day that the inspector visited in 1872, he found three boys in the schoolroom who were undergoing sentences for absconding from a reformatory. He disapproved. These boys, he wrote,

> should only be taught in their cells, and their imprisonment should be made as irksome as possible, they should also be made to work at picking oakum or breaking stones, so that indolent boys who do not like work

in a reformatory should be made to feel that prison is not a place of ease.[121]

Complete separation of young from old offenders was often difficult to achieve in the smaller local gaols, where the increasingly low numbers of juveniles made it less worthwhile to invest in the infrastructure and staffing required to implement classification. In Armagh gaol in 1870 the inspector visited the chapel, which was being used for the school, just as the prisoners were finishing their lessons, and he remarked that he 'never, even in some of the ill-managed prisons of the west, saw anything to compare with the irregularity caused by the crowding together of

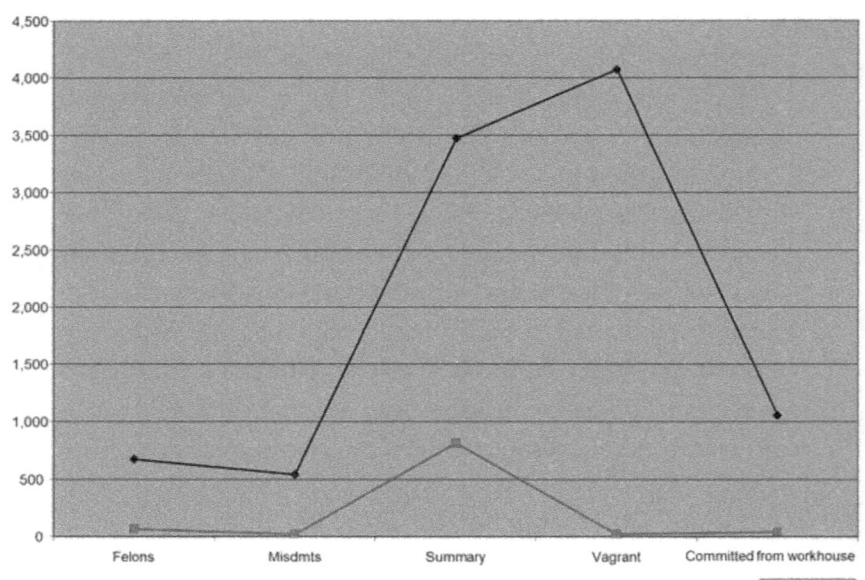

Table 3: Categories of child prisoners, 1854 and 1869

a number of men and boys'.[122] This 'crowding together' of children and adults in prison continued to give rise to concern that younger offenders would be contaminated by contact with those found guilty of serious offences. The secretary of Upton reformatory told a government enquiry that boys who came to his school told the staff about 'things they have seen and heard in prison that it had been better for them to have never known'.[123]

The range of offences for which prisoners – children as well as adults – were held in the local gaols varied greatly. The national figures from the inspectors' reports classified them as felons, misdemeanants,[124] those tried 'summarily' in the lower courts, vagrants and those prosecuted by the workhouses.

The practice of imprisoning vagrants and beggars had declined considerably since the post-Famine years.[125] This did not mean that destitution and large numbers of people who were 'wandering abroad' no longer existed. In 1868, when the judicial statistics recorded 3,680 'Vagrants and tramps' aged under sixteen,[126] there were only twenty-nine committals to prison of children for vagrancy.[127] Fourteen years earlier, over 4,000 children had been imprisoned as vagrants.[128] Changes in the manner of dealing with children will have influenced prosecutions. For example, the practice of trying children summarily became more acceptable, and the existence of the reformatories may have had an impact on sentencing practices. There may also have been a growing reluctance amongst the judiciary to imprison children, but interpretation of these statistics is, in part, 'conjectural'.[129]

The broad categories of felons, misdemeanants, and those tried summarily do not reveal much about the types of crimes for which individual prisoners had been committed. More detailed information on prisoners and their crimes can be gleaned from the prison registers and from newspaper accounts of trials. A survey of two prison registers, one from Dublin and one from Galway, shows that, of the 341 children imprisoned between 1870 and 1874, one-third had been arrested for theft.[130] The items stolen varied considerably, as did the sentencing practices of judges and magistrates. At Green Street court on the same day in 1873, young Sarah Anne Higgins was found not guilty, then guilty, on two charges of having stolen large amounts of silk. In the first case she had brought forty yards of the material to a pawnbroker. Sarah Anne said that she had gotten the stolen goods from a woman who was then brought to the court. Sarah Anne was found not guilty. She was then charged with having stolen seventy yards of silk from another shop which she also attempted to pawn. She was found guilty and sentenced to two weeks in Grangegorman and five years in the Ballinasloe reformatory.[131] Ten-year-old Robert Johnson spent fourteen days in the Galway gaol and five years in Rehoboth Place for stealing geraniums. Thirteen-year-old John D[unlea] was given the same sentence in Dublin for stealing a horse. It was frequently the victims of the child thieves who prosecuted them. 'A Dublin dairy man' brought his employee, ten-year-old Michael Farrington, to court for stealing £300. When Michael was arrested, the money was found in his pocket.[132] A Nenagh doctor prosecuted a small boy called John Haugh for stealing gooseberries from his garden. He told the court that he did not want to have him severely punished. Two of the magistrates wanted John to be sent to a reformatory for five years. A solicitor who was in court told the bench that John was the son of a poor widow and asked to have him dealt with lightly. He was sentenced to fourteen days' imprisonment with hard labour.[133] While the theft of small amounts of food would suggest that poverty was the motivation, in many cases the items that children stole were valuable.

The second most common crime for which children in the Dublin and Galway cohort were imprisoned was assault. Of the 341, eighty were found guilty of this offence. The registers, in most cases, do not describe the severity or nature of the assaults. Two boys who served sentences in the Dublin gaol for more serious crimes of physical violence were fifteen-year-old Patrick Keane, who was imprisoned for manslaughter, and James Faulkes, who was sixteen and found guilty of assaulting the police. Fifteen-year-old C[orneliu]s Galvin was given twelve months' imprisonment with hard labour for 'Aiding in a rape'.[134] Newspaper reports of trials provide more detail on the circumstances of some assaults. A young Cork boy, Michael Foster, attacked his mother with a stone and threatened to kill her in 1873. He was sent to Upton for five years. 'Wild looking' Patrick Cronin was sentenced to three years in a reformatory by a Tralee court in 1876 for an indecent assault on a six-year-old 'delicate looking' girl.[135]

Cases of murder and manslaughter perpetrated by children, while infrequent, do from time to time appear in the prison registers and in newspaper articles. Twelve-year-old Teresa Kenefick [Kenefen] was committed to Galway gaol in March 1867 for the crime of murder of an infant. She was the daughter of a coastguard officer stationed at Roundstone and was imprisoned with her sister Margaret, 'one of them having borne a child to a policeman stationed there'. The two girls were set free by the assize court in Galway later that year.[136] This was not unusual. Elaine Farrell has shown that women tried for infanticide in the nineteenth century were often treated with leniency by the courts.[137] Catherine Lavelle was charged, along with her mother and brother, with having killed her father. All were found guilty, but the jury 'recommended [Catherine] to mercy, on the ground that she had been influenced by her mother'. Catherine, who was fifteen, was given a sentence of ten years' penal servitude by Baron Fitzgerald, which was the same sentence as that given to her brother, but shorter than that of her mother, who was sentenced to life imprisonment.[138] Joseph Murray shot his friend Denis Conolly [Conneely] in the face with his father's gun in County Galway in 1885. Denis died nine hours later and Joseph was arrested. Joseph, who was twelve years old, was released on bail after a court found that the shooting was 'foolish and accidental'.[139] Peter Ahern appeared before Cork spring assizes in March 1878 charged with the manslaughter of his friend James Power. Peter, who was 'aged about twelve years', had quarrelled with James at a 'game of hurly'. He pleaded guilty and the judge released him 'on his own recognisances to come up when called on'.[140]

Young John O'Brien attacked his co-worker with a shovel while both of them were drunk in the cellar of the pub in which they worked in Limerick in 1873.[141] Alcohol often played a part in the lives and crimes of children and their families. Fourteen-year-old James Whelan was given a reformatory sentence of five years having been found 'almost insensible' after drinking a stolen bottle of wine.[142] Children who were visibly drunk and unsupervised on the streets of Dublin were a cause for concern amongst officials and the public, and it was thought that Dublin had a disproportionately high number of such children. Charles Bourke, Lentaigne's fellow inspector-general, wrote that:

> No one can walk through the streets of Dublin without observing the large number of children at all times of the day, and even at night, who appear to have no means of employment, who attend no schools, and whose parents appear to have no control for good over them.

In the female prison he found one child who was serving her eleventh sentence for drunkenness, and others serving their seventh, ninth and tenth.[143] Newspaper reports also reveal instances of children drinking in public houses, and not just in Dublin. Two boys, named by a Mayo newspaper as 'Rush and Grimes', and aged 'about eight and ten years', were found drinking in a bar in Ballinrobe, having earlier been seen breaking into a house where a sum of money was taken.[144]

Cases of child prostitution are rarely directly referenced in the prison registers but, on occasion, come to light in court cases and newspaper accounts of trials. In Galway in 1881 three young girls from the 'classic region' of Shell Lane were arrested. A newspaper which reported on the trial wrote that they 'were in the habit of making a practice of inviting all soldiers and sailors passing by to join in the merry dance'.[145] In 1875 a girl was brought to court in Dublin for absconding from High Park reformatory. She had earned her reformatory sentence having been prosecuted by her father for theft in order to 'have her taken away from an improper house on the Grand Canal'.[146] Brian Griffin describes the case of a young Belfast girl who was arrested for disorderly conduct, a crime often associated with prostitution. The arresting policeman told the court that she was 'one of ten or eleven "little girls"' who lived in a brothel run by Anthony McMahon and his wife who lived on the earnings of the girls, including his own daughters.[147] From the 1860s the judicial statistics also included numbers of prostitutes under the age of sixteen.

The remaining children in the Galway and Dublin registers found themselves in gaol for a variety of crimes which included trespass (20), illegal fishing (11), burglary (8), and cutting trees and shrubs or stealing timber (8). Five children were serving sentences for absconding from institutions. Eleven-year-old John Sullivan absconded from a Dublin workhouse where both his parents were resident. Absconders were prosecuted by the workhouse authorities for leaving with workhouse property, usually clothes. John's 'sentence' was to be returned to the institution. Richard O'Connell, who was thirteen, was arrested in Galway for absconding from Philipstown reformatory. A different type of absconding for which children were frequently prosecuted at this time was for leaving employment, either formal apprenticeships or 'service'. Eleven such children from the Dublin and Galway registers served sentences, usually one month's imprisonment, and were prosecuted by their employers. In some cases children left because they felt they were being overworked. Young Peter Mack was summoned by his boss to appear at Roscommon petty sessions in 1863 for leaving his employment. Mack told the court that he was expected to work 'late and early' and on Sundays. He was ordered to 'end his time or go to gaol for two months'.[148]

In the year ending March 1880 there were 1,255 committals of children to local gaols.[149] What these numbers, and other criminal statistics, do not reveal is the 'dark figure' of crime. This refers to the number of crimes which were not reported or not recorded. Many of the children who were gaoled were brought to court by their victims, but some victims may have chosen not to prosecute. Police may also have dealt with young offenders themselves, either by meting out a spontaneous corporal punishment, or by dealing with an offending child's parents, or by ignoring a petty offence. One magistrate who sat at one of the busiest courts in the country said that he often imposed a fine on a child criminal knowing that if the parents had to pay they would 'give the child a good flogging'. External factors also had an effect on how crime was dealt with and subsequently recorded. After the establishment of the reformatories, some sympathetic magistrates 'softened down' the crimes of children, especially girls, so that they would be sent to industrial schools and not reformatories. In such cases the criminal statistics would not record a crime where one had occurred or would record a less serious offence.[150]

Those who campaigned for the establishment of a reformatory school system in Ireland hoped that these new institutions would provide an alternative to imprisonment for young offenders. However, despite the opening of ten schools, and provision for younger offenders in industrial schools, judges and magistrates continued to send children to gaol two decades after the passing of the act of 1858. Some policemen or court officials, like Furlong's 'good and worthy magistrate', may have been sympathetic to the parents of children, or the children themselves, who did not want to be sent to a reformatory. The sentences were considerably longer than gaol sentences, usually five years, and the reformatories were often a long distance from the child's home. Many children at the time made important contributions to the family livelihood. Some magistrates may have been opposed in principle to the new schools on the grounds of their cost to the Treasury and local authority, or on religious grounds. The 'short, sharp shock' of a couple of days or a week in a local gaol may have been considered a sufficient deterrent. Meanwhile, momentum was growing internationally to remove children from the adult penal system. There was a renewed focus on achieving this in Ireland by the end of the nineteenth century.

Chapter 4

Saving Children from 'Moral Ruin': 1880–1908

BY THE EARLY 1880s circumstances for many of Ireland's poor and criminal children had altered considerably. The proportion of young people in workhouses had almost halved since the 1850s,[1] and the numbers in industrial schools continued to rise. Although reformatories had been established as an alternative to imprisonment, and the numbers of children in them peaked at this time, Irish courts still favoured gaol over the new institutions for criminal children. In 1883 the Catholic chaplain of Richmond bridewell told a government enquiry that imprisonment of children with adults resulted in irreparable 'moral ruin',[2] an opinion which was shared by most observers. Over the next three decades, new laws concerning the treatment of children convicted of crime were debated and enacted, with a particular focus on removing children from the adult criminal justice system. One of the first of these was a law designed to change the way that courts dealt with children.

Children in court

Bridget Galvin was ten years old when she was sent by her employer to the post office in Gort in County Galway to cash two post office orders. Her employer accused her of stealing the money. At her trial at the Galway assizes in March 1854, Bridget cried and protested her innocence. She was found not guilty of the offence by the jury and walked free, but she had served two months' imprisonment in Galway gaol while waiting to be tried in the higher court.[3] When an inspector visited the same gaol twenty years later, he was troubled to find a barefoot young girl running around in the company of women who were repeat offenders. The girl was in gaol awaiting trial and the inspector wrote that she might have been 'perfectly innocent'.[4] Between April 1883 and March 1884, twenty-seven children under twelve years of age and 190 between the ages of twelve and sixteen who were 'not convicted and untried' were held in local gaols.[5]

The solution that was proposed to deal with this issue was to try children summarily for more serious offences in the lower courts. In 1884 a bill was brought before parliament to extend to Ireland further measures for summary jurisdiction over children. Some Irish members of parliament argued against the increased powers which the bill would give to police and magistrates, in particular the power to inflict corporal punishment. Their arguments were made in the context of heightened tensions due to land agitation and changing attitudes to cruelty to children. In the parliamentary debate William O'Brien, MP for Mallow, declared that he would 'not care to find that the child of an Irish tenant could be whipped by a policeman for whistling *Harvey Duff*, or for some such trifling delinquency', while Charles Stewart Parnell referred to 'the barbarous punishment of flogging'. O'Brien was referring to an alleged assault with a bayonet on a twelve-year-old girl in Limerick by a policeman for singing a 'seditious' song. Edward Gibson, who supported the bill, said that he would prefer to see his own child whipped than sent to prison for a month. Their opinions reflected a wider debate in Britain where whipping of juvenile offenders was widely supported as an alternative to imprisonment but there was disagreement over who should inflict the punishment.[6]

The Summary Jurisdiction over Children Act (Ireland) became law in July 1884.[7] The act made a clear distinction between 'children' under twelve years of age, and 'young persons' who were aged above twelve and under sixteen. Under the new law, children who were brought to court for any crime other than homicide could, with the permission of their parents or guardians, be tried by the lower courts of petty sessions or police courts. The possible sentences were, consequently, reduced to imprisonment of not more than a month, a fine of no more than forty shillings, and, for boys, six strokes of a birch rod administered in the presence of a senior officer and the child's parents. Young persons charged with a range of offences could be sentenced to up to three months in prison, a fine of up to £10, or twelve strokes if they were under the age of fourteen.[8] A year after the passing of the new law, only fifteen children, all boys, were serving sentences in the local gaols having been tried at quarter sessions and assizes, compared with 651 who had been tried summarily.[9]

Magistrates were often criticised for the arbitrary nature of their sentencing, especially when it came to children. Because the reformatory legislation was permissive, one child found guilty of a crime could be sent to an institution for five years, while another guilty of the same crime could serve a week in a local gaol or not be prosecuted at all. Sir William Harcourt, the home secretary, believed that many children were sent to reformatories for some crimes which he considered 'petty act[s] of naughtiness (such as our own children commit every day)'. He asked that he be personally informed of all cases of children under the age of fifteen who were sent to prison and asked magistrates to look for alternatives to imprisonment for children.[10] In 1875 an English prison governor described the unevenness of sentencing as 'a kind of lottery'.[11] In Britain the severity of some reformatory sentences was brought to the attention of government. Four years after Robert Johnson was sentenced in Galway to five years in a reformatory for stealing geraniums, a remarkably similar case occurred in Lincolnshire. Twelve-year-old Sarah Chandler was given a reformatory sentence for the crime of 'wilful damage to a geranium plant'. Sarah, like Robert, was a first offender, and the harshness of her sentence led the home secretary to issue a 'severe rebuke' to the magistrate.[12]

Reformers also turned their attention to young petty offenders, especially those who had not been convicted before. In Massachusetts a system of probation for young offenders had been introduced which claimed great success in halting the criminal careers of young, first-time criminals. Variations of the system were promoted in Britain by the Howard Association and by Howard Vincent, a lawyer and MP. In 1887 the Probation of First Offenders Act was passed.[13] It made provision for any first offender 'convicted of larceny or false pretences, or any other offence punishable with not more than two years imprisonment', 'regard being had to [their] youth, character and antecedents' to be released on probation. The response to the legislation in Ireland disappointed some in the criminal justice system, and, yet again, magistrates were blamed. In 1892 a circular was issued reminding them of the provisions of the act. The prison inspectors reported that 11,694 committals in 1890–1 were of first offenders (both adults and children), yet the probation act was only used in 232 cases in the previous year. They cited the case of a little girl of twelve who was arrested and brought to prison for larceny and was so terrified that she was 'almost in a state of collapse'. 'But still we find', they wrote, 'that little children are sometimes committed to prison, and a mark of infamy placed upon them for life ... cases which to our mind would be more profitably dealt with under the Probation of First Offenders Act'. Three juvenile first offenders had their sentences overturned in 1891–2.[14] One of these was a ten-year-old schoolboy from County Tipperary, William Dee. William had been given a sentence of fourteen days in gaol and two years in Philipstown for the crime of 'Injuring [an] electric telegraph wire' by throwing missiles at it. Following the intervention of the chief justices, he was released after his fourteen days in gaol.[15]

While the probation act was applicable to all first offenders, it was felt that extra measures were needed in the case of children, and the Youthful Offenders Act of 1901 extended the range of probation for young people.[16] Some courts began to treat young first-time criminals more leniently. When young Nannie Downes appeared in court for breaking into and stealing from a house with her older brother, he was sent to a reformatory, while the bench discharged her as a first offender, believing that she had been 'led into it by him'.[17] Two young boys were given the benefit of the legislation for the crime of firing at a goods train in Newtownmountkennedy in 1902.[18]

Some magistrates, however, continued to give custodial sentences to first offenders. Patrick McKenna was fifteen years old when he was accused at Enniskillen petty sessions of stealing a cash box from his employer. Although he had never been in trouble before, and his employer asked for leniency for him, the bench decided to send him to Glencree for three years, telling him that he would be 'well taken care of and taught a trade'. Both Patrick and his mother wept during the trial. The newspaper that reported the case ran it under the headline 'Youth Sent to a Reformatory for a First Offence'.[19] It was not until 1907, however, that the Probation of Offenders Act[20] 'effected a great reformation' and provided Ireland with a more workable system. One probation officer, Kathleen Gargan, was appointed after the enactment. She was assisted by an 'unpaid volunteer', Miss O'Brien. The Dublin Metropolitan Police reported that sixty-eight boys and eleven girls were subject to probation orders in the first year of the operation of the law.[21] Despite this perceived progress, however, Paul Sargent has noted that 'no formal probation service developed' outside Dublin following the 1907 legislation.[22]

Described as a 'watershed event' in child welfare,[23] the Children Act of 1908 was a wide-ranging piece of legislation. It brought together and amended many aspects of the criminal justice system as it applied to children.[24] One of the purposes of the legislation was to ensure that the child offender 'should receive at the hands of the law a treatment differentiated to suit his special needs – that the courts should be agencies for the rescue as well as the punishment of children'.[25] The 'Act to consolidate and amend the Law relating to the Protection of Children and Young Persons, Reformatory and Industrial Schools, and Juvenile Offenders, and otherwise to amend the Law with respect to Children and Young Persons' ran to seventy-six pages on the statute books. It abolished the death penalty for children and provided a range of alternatives where a child was found guilty of an offence, from dismissal, to probation, to a sentence in a reformatory or industrial school. It is, perhaps, most frequently associated with the establishment of separate courts for children. Section 111 of the act stated that courts of summary jurisdiction should sit in a separate room or building, or on different days, when children were being tried.[26]

The Philanthropic Reform Association (PRA) had been campaigning for a separate court for children in Dublin since at least 1904. In October of that year the *Irish Daily Independent* reported that '[i]t is greatly to the credit of Dublin that it should be the first city in the United Kingdom to provide a separate court for the hearing of criminal charges against juveniles', although the association subsequently expressed its dissatisfaction with the arrangement and sought hearings in a separate building.[27] The act of 1908 looked to precedents in Norway, the

United States, Australia and Canada. A growing awareness of issues of child welfare meant that the act passed through parliament in London 'on oiled wheels'.[28]

On the inside

By the late nineteenth century the drive to remove children, especially the very young, from the prison system was gaining widespread support internationally. In Ireland the proportion of juvenile to adult prisoners had fallen considerably by 1880. The 1,255 committals of children formed only 3 per cent of prisoners in 1880, compared with nearly 18 per cent in 1854, but there was agreement that further measures were needed. It was not just the welfare of the children and the possible 'contamination' from older prisoners that concerned reformers. It was also thought that children who were imprisoned early in life lost their fear of imprisonment. The chaplain of Belfast gaol described the case of a boy who was sent there from the country. When first imprisoned, 'he shrank from everybody in fear and trembling, and wept bitterly', but two weeks later told the chaplain that it was not such a bad place because people were kind and nobody beat him.[29]

This was a period of closure and consolidation in the Irish prison system. Between 1877 and 1887, seventy-seven bridewells and twelve local gaols closed. In 1888 Richmond bridewell, the great Dublin gaol that had been the scene of such misery and chaos after the Famine, closed. In 1894 a government inquiry into the prison system, the Gladstone Committee,[30] was established in response to criticism of British prisons, and in 1896 new rules for the treatment of incarcerated juveniles were implemented. All children under sixteen years of age who were serving sentences of more than a month were now to be sent to either Grangegorman or Mountjoy gaols. Those serving shorter sentences in local gaols would be kept completely separate from adult prisoners. The dreaded plank bed[31] could no longer be used for children, and they were to be allowed special library books, additional training in trades, and outdoor exercise. Chaplains were to devote particular attention to young prisoners, and they were also to be allowed extra visits, if it was thought that these would improve their 'moral welfare and future career'.[32] Three years later, the nineteen male and four female prisoners who had been sent to Mountjoy under the new regime were reported to be doing well, with the girls gardening and the boys showing an improvement in their physiques.[33]

Outside of officialdom, public awareness of child welfare was increasing thanks to newly formed organisations like the National Society for the Prevention of Cruelty to Children (NSPCC) and the PRA, and to prominent individuals such as Oscar Wilde. In 1897 he was so moved by the children he had seen while incarcerated in Reading gaol that he wrote a long letter to the editor of the *Daily Chronicle* which was subsequently published as a pamphlet. His description of what he witnessed was stark and poignant. While the main catalyst for his letter was reading in the *Chronicle* that a warder from Reading had been sacked for giving a very small hungry boy a biscuit, a boy that Wilde had seen being admitted to the prison before his own release, he also articulated extensive criticism of the English prison system with regard to children. He believed that separate confinement of children, in particular, traumatised them, and described seeing a boy whose face was 'like a white wedge of sheer terror', and who was crying out for his parents after a night spent alone in his cell. Perhaps most interestingly, he wrote that the 'contamination' of children in gaol came from the system itself, while it was the prisoners who showed kindness and humanity to each other. The little boy who was given the biscuit was imprisoned with two other children. Wilde wrote that '[t]here is not a single man in Reading gaol that would not gladly have done the three children's punishment for them'. He believed that no child under the age of fourteen should be imprisoned.

Prison officials and reformers had been drawing attention to the plight of child prisoners for many years, but their descriptions were buried in official reports, rarely read by the public. Wilde's letter and pamphlet vividly brought the matter into the public domain.[34] In the same year, the city coroner for Dublin told a public meeting that, while on a visit to Kilmainham gaol, he heard cries coming from a cell which, he was told, held children serving their fourteen-day preliminary sentences before being sent to a reformatory. He discovered that they were being 'grossly ill-treated', spoke to the governor, and had the abuse stopped.[35]

When, in their report of 1892, the General Prisons Board expressed their frustration that young children were still being sent to gaol despite the many provisions to prevent it, they were echoing that of their predecessors who, for many years, had been highlighting the gap that existed between the passing of legislation and its implementation. While the 1901 Youthful Offenders Act gave courts the power to place a child or young person with 'any fit person ... who is willing to receive him' instead of prison while awaiting trial, some courts continued to ignore the new laws. In 1905 ten boys and two girls under twelve years of age were imprisoned in Ireland, including a seven-year-old boy who was remanded in Galway gaol while awaiting trial for travelling on the train without a ticket, using abusive language, and assault. In 1906 the board expressed their regret that such young children were still being sent to gaol by magistrates when there were so many alternatives available to them. These children would, they wrote, be 'branded with the Prison taint, and being well and kindly treated, lose the salutary dread of Prison'.[36]

In 1908 the Prisons Board presented a table showing the numbers of children committed to prison in the previous ten years. They wrote that the practice of imprisoning the very young had been 'almost given up'. In 1907 five boys under twelve years of age were imprisoned. In three of the previous four years no girls in the same age category were sent to gaol. The board singled out the case of a ten-year-old boy who was sent to Birr bridewell for twenty-four hours for the crime of hurling in the street. They wrote that they hoped that 'an effectual stop will soon be put to the committal of children of tender years to prison, as the "Children's Bill" now before parliament' made it illegal.[37]

This long piece of legislation dealt with the incarceration of children in one short phrase: 'A child shall not be sentenced to imprisonment or penal servitude for any offence.' Young persons could no longer be sentenced to penal servitude and could only be imprisoned if they were of so 'unruly' and 'depraved' a character that there was no alternative.[38]

Preliminary imprisonment of children before their reformatory sentence had always been contentious. It was abolished by a short piece of legislation in 1899 which stated that an offender sentenced to a reformatory 'shall not in addition be sentenced to penal servitude or imprisonment',[39] which had the support of the PRA. They met at the home of the recorder of Dublin, Frederick Falkiner, in May 1900.[40] Falkiner's interest in poor and criminal children was not new. In 1883 he had given evidence to the members of a government enquiry that had travelled to Ireland to investigate industrial schools and reformatories. The enquiry had come about because of public disquiet at the administration of the schools in Britain. The institutional model was beginning to be questioned, and the treatment of the children within the institutions was gaining unfavourable attention from those interested in child welfare.

Unrest amongst inmates, which sometimes spilled outside the gates into abscondings, harsh punishments and the exploitation and abuse of children in some industrial schools in Britain, forced the government to take action. Some public figures in Britain regarded reformatories and industrial schools as 'a system of organised and legalised philanthropic kidnapping', while a Home Office investigation concluded that there were children in both institutions 'who ought never to have been sent there, or who have been sent there too early, or who are kept there too long'.[41] In 1882 the government in London responded to complaints regarding the institutions by establishing an enquiry.

The Royal Commission to Investigate the Reformatory and Industrial Schools was chaired by Lord Aberdare, and its members included Sir Michael Hicks-Beach, former chief secretary of Ireland, and the O'Conor Don. In January 1883 they were amongst nine members of the commission that travelled to Ireland. They sat in Belfast, Dublin, Kilkenny and Cork and took evidence from over forty witnesses, as well as inspecting eight reformatories and nineteen industrial schools,[42] exhibiting 'scrupulous fidelity' to their duty in their inspections.[43] They called public officials, clerics, members of the judiciary, and reformatory and industrial school managers, as well as members of the public, as witnesses, and questioned them about the 'operation, management, control, inspection, financial arrangements, and condition generally' of the institutions.[44] On 26 January 1883, the commission first sat in the council chamber in Belfast.

David Barclay, the governor of Malone reformatory, was called to give evidence. Lord Aberdare observed that very few boys were sent out on licence from Malone. Barclay's answer was that 'every institution dependent upon the Capitation grant must endeavour to keep up its numbers'. The commission remarked on the fact that the industrial profits from Malone were comparatively high and questioned Barclay on the type of training given to the boys and whether it prepared them for life outside the school. Lord Aberdare noted the comparatively high number of first offenders, and of children of a 'tender age' who were sent to reformatories in Ireland. He observed that out of 269 boys sent to reformatories in 1881, 225 were first offenders and seventy-one were under the age of twelve. Without them, he said, there would have been 'very little for the reformatories to do in Ireland'.[45] After a day of taking evidence, the members of the commission packed their bags and left Belfast for Dublin, stopping along the way to visit Spark's Lake.

On 31 January 1883, they sat at City Hall, Dublin, where Frederick Falkiner gave evidence. Known as 'the poor man's judge',[46] he showed remarkable sympathy for the people who appeared in his court. He quoted to the commission from an enquiry which showed that 30,000 people in Dublin were living in tenements that were unfit for human habitation. One effect of this, Falkiner said, was to drive people out onto the streets:

> Life is not a lovely thing in the squalid room of the squalid tenement house ... usually the only joy of life is strong drink, bought at the cost of what would make the home habitable ... the children, passing an unchildlike childhood, take prematurely to the streets.[47]

These children led hard lives, according to Falkiner, enduring 'some strange sort of struggle for existence', 'eking out' a life that was akin to vagrancy. While denying that this was a criminal class, he conceded that they did resort to criminality, which sometimes included violence. He believed that the solution for such children was to establish day industrial schools where the children might be taught trades and basic literary education during the day, returning to their homes at night. For many children who were found begging on the streets, Falkiner said, it was thought to be a 'cruel thing' to hand them over to a policeman. He told the commission that when a criminal child appeared before him he always asked to see the parents. Unlike many of the advocates of the industrial and reformatory schools who believed that criminal children should always be removed from their homes and placed in institutions, Falkiner was of the belief that even a 'wretched' home was still a home, and children who returned home from day industrial schools might become 'night missionaries of order and sobriety' whose parents would be 'elevated' by their influence.

On the subject of reformatories, the recorder said that he saw many former inmates appear before him, and he went so far as to say that many habitual criminals 'commenced in reformatories' and led others into crime. Where very young boys were brought to his court, he believed that it was a 'positive cruelty' to send them to prison or a reformatory, and he had asked the police to bring such boys from his court to the lower courts 'under any qualification that they could get for him'. Many of these young children were tried along with older children. He gave the example of groups of children who came before him for stealing lead from roofs. Some in the group would be first offenders, but he often found that one was an older 'Glencree boy'. He was in favour of greater government involvement in the running of the reformatories, believing that inspection by one man, John Lentaigne, was not enough.[48]

The commissioners put the eighty-year-old Lentaigne, by now Sir John, through the most arduous session of all of the witnesses, putting 374 questions to him over the course of the day. He said that he had made twenty-two visits to the ten reformatories in the previous year, usually unannounced. As with other witnesses, the inspector was questioned about the large proportion of very young children and first offenders in Irish reformatory schools. He told the commission that he believed that a boy under twelve years of age should only be sent to a reformatory under exceptional circumstances, and that he had found 150 such young boys in the three big Catholic reformatories in 1880. Lentaigne was asked by the O'Conor Don whether he thought excessive punishment was used in the reformatories. He answered that he thought not and handed in a table compiled from information supplied by the school managers, detailing numbers of offences committed by inmates and the most severe punishments meted out in 1882.[49]

The table provides extraordinary detail on the range and extent of punishment in the schools. In Rehoboth a boy who had absconded was made to work with a ten-pound iron shot tied to his leg with a five-foot chain, while in Philipstown boys were forced to carry pack drill for three days. In Upton, Glencree and Philipstown boys who were punished had their hair cut. Although the regime in Ballinasloe, as reported by the manager, would appear to have been much milder than in the other schools, with no corporal punishment, separation of children in punishment cells was still used. Glencree boys faced up to five days in solitary confinement. In High Park the cell was only resorted to in the daytime, but children could spend up to eleven days confined there.

The extent and frequency of corporal punishments varied greatly within the schools. The Whipping of Offenders Act of 1862 provided for a maximum of twelve strokes with a birch to be imposed by the courts.[50] No such limits would appear to have been enforced inside the institutions. In Malone reformatory boys were given up to eighteen lashes. Boys in Philipstown endured up to twenty-one strokes with a birch rod. Girls in High Park were given up to twenty 'stripes', while the Cork Street girls were slapped with a tawse (a thong with a slit end). Limerick girls were given five slaps on their hands, while those in Spark's Lake got a 'slight whipping' and 'a few slaps'. The frequency of punishments inflicted in one reformatory stands out from all of the others. While Ballinasloe, Limerick and Monaghan reported that offences punished were 'very few', Upton reported that there were 434 punishments meted out for offences committed by its 227 inmates in 1882. These were the punishments that were reported by the reformatory managers. It is likely that there were others that went unreported.

Lentaigne was asked what effect he believed the reformatory and industrial schools had on crime in Ireland. His response was to cite the crime statistics from thirty years earlier, the same figures from the early 1850s that Murray had used to support his case for the establishment of the reformatory system. Lentaigne compared the figures to those for 1881. In an extraordinary exchange between the inspector and Lord Aberdare, the chairman asked whether Lentaigne believed that it was the institutions, and not the poverty that resulted from the Famine and a diminution of population of three million people, that accounted for this decrease in crime.[51] The inspector was using the post-Famine crime figures to claim success for the reformatories. Such manipulation of criminal statistics is consistent with discussions of whether juvenile delinquency was an 'invention' in this period.[52]

On 7 February 1883 the commission dismissed their last witness in Cork and returned to England to prepare their report for parliament. It was published in 1884. The report concluded that the twin institutions in Britain had a 'very satisfactory' effect on the reduction in crime but suggested that the British establishments could benefit from copying two aspects of the Irish system. They recommended that more British schools should have women as managers and visitors and cited the example of the Irish schools run by nuns where the girls were 'under the care of refined and educated women'. They also referred to the desirability of a penal reformatory for refractory children in Britain and suggested Spark's Lake in Monaghan as a model which might successfully be replicated. Lord Norton, a member of the commission, disagreed. He called penal reformatory schools 'a contradiction in terms', saying that the reformatory and industrial school system had been 'warped ... from its true intention'.[53]

In their recommendations on Ireland, the commissioners wrote that they were 'unable to trace in Ireland the influence of these institutions on crime, whether juvenile or adult' as clearly as they had done for Britain. They noted that one of the most 'striking' features of the Irish reformatory system was the large number of very young children in the schools who had been committed for 'trifling offences'. They singled out Glencree, Philipstown and Upton as having a larger proportion of such inmates. If 'genuine reformatory cases' were not sufficient to fill the schools, they recommended that more schools like the Kilmore probationary industrial school be opened instead of reformatories, or other measures be taken to rectify the situation. In what must have been a snub to John Lentaigne, they referred to the dramatic decrease in population and social 'disturbances' such as the Famine, and their impact on crime. They wrote that '[t]he effects of the reformatory schools on the character and conduct of the children committed to them were much contested'. They questioned the figures given to them by John Lentaigne regarding crimes committed by former reformatory inmates and cited figures which showed that in the five years ending in 1881 there were 846 committals to gaol of males and 240 of females who had been in reformatory schools.[54] They did, however, later concede that the industrial and reformatory schools had saved large numbers of children from a life of crime. Overall, the commissioners expressed their admiration for the way that most of the Irish schools were run, especially those for girls. They added:

> We should be sorry to be thought insensible to the zealous and humane efforts of those who are charged with the management of the boys' reformatory schools. The reformatory school at Philipstown especially appears to be in all respects excellently conducted.[55]

John Lentaigne resigned in 1886, giving his 'advanced age, and the constantly increasing number of schools' as his reason. In his final report he, like his predecessor Murray, declared himself satisfied with an institutional system that he had become so closely associated with, a system that he believed had taken 'firm root' in Ireland.[56] He died in November of that year, at the age of eighty-two. The boys of the Artane industrial school marched in his funeral cortege to Glasnevin cemetery.[57]

His office was filled temporarily by F.X.F. MacCabe from the General Prisons Board, and then for the next three years by George Plunkett O'Farrell. In his first detailed report in 1889, Plunkett O'Farrell noted that no legislative reforms had yet been enacted as a result of the Aberdare Commission's recommendations. He went on to list his own observations on the changes he would like to see. The first was a prohibition on children under twelve being sent to reformatories unless the child had been 'so perverted by habitual crime as to render his detention in an Industrial School a source of danger to its other inmates'.[58] Despite its perceived success, the probationary school at Kilmore closed in 1889 and became an ordinary industrial school, owing, the inspector wrote, to the 'scarcity' of young boys to fill it, even though fifty-nine children under the age of twelve had been sent to reformatories in the previous year.[59] Barnes has noted that 'observers were puzzled at the failure of Kilmore'.[60]

Upton also closed as a reformatory in 1889 and the school was recertified as an industrial school. Its 123 inmates were transferred to Philipstown and Glencree. They became the only reformatories for Catholic boys in Ireland and had, after the closure of Upton, 280 inmates each.[61] Plunkett O'Farrell's successor, Rowland Blennerhassett, was fulsome in his praise of Philipstown, where the brothers were 'unceasing in their labours to make [the] lads good Christians' while leaving 'nothing undone to provide them with the means of earning an honest livelihood as skilful tradesmen'. He had less to say about Glencree, where two boys had stood trial for serious assaults on a member of staff and another inmate.[62] As the nineteenth century drew to a close, the numbers in Philipstown increased as those in Glencree decreased. In 1908 a head constable asked a court to send two boys accused of stealing a purse to Glencree, stating that there were '50 vacancies' there.[63] In the schools for girls the numbers of admissions were so low that John Fagan, who replaced Blennerhassett, recommended in 1902 that there should only be one reformatory for Catholic girls for all of Ireland. By this time, High Park had twenty-three inmates, and Limerick and Spark's Lake had nineteen each.[64] A district inspector asked another court to send a girl to High Park, telling the bench that he had a letter from the manager of the school telling him that she had 'several vacancies'.[65] The Monaghan school, founded by the indomitable Genevieve Beale in 1859, closed in 1903.

The story of the Protestant reformatories in the late nineteenth century was also one of declining numbers. The only reformatory for Protestant girls, Cork Street, closed in 1895. Although there were so few girls being given reformatory sentences that it was not considered financially viable to keep an institution open, the inspector worried for the welfare of those who no longer had the chance to be sent to a reformatory. Protestant girls were being sent to gaol by the judiciary, thereby 'ignoring the possibility of reformation'.[66] Malone in Belfast became the only Protestant reformatory in Ireland. When young Jacob Swiney was given a four-year sentence in Bandon in 1903, he faced the long journey from the south of the country to begin his time in Malone.[67]

The Children Act dealt another blow to the viability of the reformatories. Section 58 of the act consolidated previous attempts to remove children under twelve years of age from them. These young, vulnerable children that Aberdare and successive inspectors had agreed did not belong in reformatories would, in most cases, no longer be sent to them and instead, if the court was satisfied that it was 'expedient so to deal with the child', they would be sent to an industrial school. At the other end of the age range for juveniles, a new category of young offender emerged. Male criminals between the ages of sixteen and twenty-one, or 'juvenile-adults', were identified as a group that was too old for reformatories, yet not suited to adult prisons either. A borstal system, which already existed in Britain, was extended to Ireland in 1906.[68] The new institution made special provision for one aspect of institutional care that had not been sufficiently addressed up to this time – the aftercare of inmates once they had left the institutions and begun their lives in the outside world.

On the outside

The lives of Irish children changed a great deal in the half century after the Famine. They were much more likely to be at school at the start of the twentieth century, since the Education Act of 1892[69] made attendance at school compulsory. The 1901 census noted that there had been 'a continued improvement decade by decade' of literacy levels: 94 per cent of children between the ages of ten and fifteen could read and write, compared with 59 per cent thirty years earlier.[70] Attitudes to children were changing too, bolstered by legislation such as the Infant Life Protection Act of 1872 and the Prevention of Cruelty to Children Act of 1889.[71] Organisations like the PRA and the NSPCC brought issues of child poverty and neglect into the public gaze in Ireland. These groups, founded in the last decades of the nineteenth century, were influential, and the NSPCC, like the PRA, was involved in 'active lobbying for legislative change'.[72]

Despite these reforms, there were still many children for whom poverty meant that their childhoods were short-lived. Children were an important source of income for many families, but working children became the focus of reformers' attention at the turn of the century. In 1902 a government committee was formed in Dublin to investigate street trading by children. John Fagan, the inspector of reformatories, was one of its members. The committee found that there were 2,000 children trading on the streets of Belfast, Dublin and Cork. It concluded that the lives of these children were 'wretched' and that they needed 'supervision to keep them straight'.[73] The 1903 Employment of Children Act sought to regulate these street children.[74] Lord Meath, president of the PRA, claimed that his organisation was to be credited for the extension of the act to Ireland. Street trading by children was, he claimed 'often a pretext for begging', and the act would 'prove a strong factor in the prevention of juvenile crime'. The act empowered local authorities to regulate the hours that children could be on the streets and prohibited children under eleven years of age from selling on the street at any time.[75] In October 1905 seventy boys and girls were brought to a Dublin court under the terms of the act. One newspaper reported that 'none appeared deeply imbued with the majesty of the law'. The court suspended the licences of some of the young traders, but only for a 'short period'. Two members of the PRA were present in court.[76]

By the end of the nineteenth century, 8,142 children had been discharged from reformatories. On discharge, the school managers reported that the greatest proportion, just over 3,000, returned to 'friends', whereas 2,633 went to 'employment or service'.[77] Life on the outside presented many challenges for reformatory inmates who had entered the institutions and come back into society as young adults, or in some cases as children still. Finding employment for ex-reformatory inmates was often difficult for managers, and this was articulated by the secretary of Upton reformatory to the Aberdare Commission. He said that the navy would not take them, and, although some had been sent to North and South America from Upton, John Lentaigne disapproved of sending discharged inmates abroad unless a definite job awaited them. For those who stayed at home, he said, the stigma of their sentences hung over them:

We have two boys at present in Dublin that are cabinet-makers by trade and I have heard from one of the best cabinet-makers in Dublin that those two boys are able to take their stand and work with any other man in Dublin working at the bench, but unfortunately it is frequently thrown up at the boys that they have been in a reformatory, and it injures them very much, and those lads prefer to go to London where nobody would know them.[78]

Of more concern to the detractors of the reformatory system was the number of ex-reformatory inmates who reoffended. The appearance of the reoffenders in court, and comments made by members of the judiciary which were subsequently published in newspapers, harmed the reputation of the schools and stung their supporters. In January 1908 a judge told his court that 'boys sent to reformatories do not turn out very well'. In March another judge, while trying a fifty-six-year-old man, noted that he had commenced his 'calendar of crime' in a reformatory, and said that he had never sent a boy to one.[79] In 1889 the inspector, George Plunkett O'Farrell, addressed the comments of one judge who, when sentencing a young woman, remarked that she had begun her criminal career in a reformatory, 'the usual school from which criminals came'. O'Farrell wrote that former reformatory inmates doing well were never noticed, and unlikely to draw attention to their backgrounds. He believed that there would always be some incorrigible children who were beyond help. This he attributed to 'something innately bad in the individual (heredity)' and not to any defect in the schools.[80]

The support of former prisoners and reformatory inmates after they had finished their sentences was identified as a key element in preventing recidivism. In 1908 the MP Joseph Nannetti, who had been on the House of Commons committee responsible for the Children Act, said on a visit to Glencree that 'a very unsympathetic world' awaited the boys when they left the school.[81] The necessity of patronage societies to fund and oversee the welfare of those discharged from reformatories had been recognised since the establishment of the system but had never succeeded in Ireland. A society had been formed in Cork but had been disbanded due to lack of attendance of its members.[82] When the Clonmel borstal was established, aftercare became a crucial part of the young men's treatment. Every boy who left the borstal was placed in the care of a dedicated organisation, originally called the Clonmel Discharged Prisoners' Aid Society.[83] The situation was somewhat better for discharged prisoners than for reformatory inmates, and by the early twentieth century there were twelve voluntary groups looking after the welfare of former prisoners.[84]

In 1909 the inspector of reformatories wrote that the passing of the Children Act the previous year had been 'the most notable event in the history of Reformatory and Industrial Schools'.[85] The act made provision for school managers to remain responsible for their former inmates until they were nineteen years of age. In the case of a child or young person who 'conducts himself well', either on licence or after their discharge, the managers were also empowered to 'apprentice him to, or dispose of him in, any trade, calling, or service, including service in the Navy or Army, or by emigration'.[86]

In the last decades of the nineteenth century a number of measures were introduced which removed children, especially the very young and first offenders, from adult gaols. The passing of the Children Act of 1908 legislated against imprisonment of very young children and restricted its use by the courts for older children. This was a period of consolidation and closure in the Irish prison system. Reformatories were closing too as the numbers of children being sent to them decreased, so that by 1908 there were only five, and children under twelve would no longer be sent to them after the implementation of the act.[87] This wide-ranging legislation has been characterised as 'an exceptionally liberal and innovative measure for its time'.[88] It remained, in large part, 'the statutory framework upon which the system [of juvenile justice] was based for almost one hundred years'.[89] In the seven decades since the Famine committals of children who were convicted of crime in Ireland dwindled from almost 11,000 to five. The Children Act ended child imprisonment in all but the most exceptional circumstances.

Conclusion

In the 1850s thousands of Irish children were trying to survive by whatever means they could, either alone or with their families. Many of these children found themselves in gaol or the workhouse. Out of this chaotic atmosphere emerged a small but increasingly influential movement which worked towards the setting up of a reformatory system for Ireland, a system that had already been established in Britain. The great motivating influence behind the British reformers was Mary Carpenter, who believed that children should be treated as a special group within the criminal justice system. At the centre of the Irish movement was Patrick Joseph Murray, a Dublin barrister who was of the opinion that Ireland should have its own reformatory system. The Irish reformatory movement coincided with a time of great religious tension, when Protestant and Catholic agencies were establishing institutions to provide food, shelter and education to the poor. Children increasingly found themselves the focus of the missionary zeal of members of both churches. When Murray was drafting his reformatory bills he and the Irish Catholic MPs who brought them to parliament were heavily influenced by the Catholic hierarchy. The Irish Catholic Church was gaining greater influence, and its clergy was growing in number. The result was that the Reformatory Schools Act of 1858 placed a strong emphasis on the religious nature of the schools and contained provisions to ensure that children could only be sent to a school managed by members of their own religion.

The 1858 Act was permissive and relied on the discretion of judges and magistrates to decide whether a child was a fit subject for reformatory treatment. The response of the Irish judiciary reflected the sometimes conflicting attitudes of society towards criminal children. Sentences given to children were arbitrary, especially after the passing of the Reformatory Schools Act. A boy who picked up a lump of coal could be sentenced to five years, while another guilty of a more serious offence could be set free. Some judges and magistrates treated the children harshly, inflicting severe punishments for petty crimes, while others expressed sympathy for the children who appeared before them. For some, this sympathy translated into a reformatory sentence because they believed that to be removed from a difficult environment and sent to a place where they would be sheltered and trained was the best possible outcome for some children. Others, like the Dublin judge Frederick Falkiner, believed that the best place for a child was their home, even if it was a very poor one, and that children should only be sent away to an institution as a last resort. It is also possible, particularly in the early years of the reformatory system, that there was a religious dimension to sentencing. A Protestant judge or magistrate may not have been inclined to send children to a Catholic institution, and vice versa.

For some children, the schools may have been a better alternative to a hard and sometimes violent life lived eking out an existence by legal or illegal means. Many children who came to the institutions came with the 'marks of violence' already on them, and we learned in chapter 3 that violence perpetrated by children was common. But the reality of life in an institution with young children who had been removed from their families and communities must frequently have deviated greatly from the somewhat simplistic ideals of the reformers. Even Mary Carpenter struggled when it came to managing a reformatory and it has been said that she 'never succeeded in creating the kind of institution which she had advocated'.[1] Children, like adult prisoners in the nineteenth century, were subject to the 'rise and fall of optimism'.[2] The optimism of those reformers who believed that a child could be taken away from family and friends for years and moulded into an honest citizen fell away, and the public support for reformatories that they had hoped for also dwindled. Poor living conditions, hard physical labour and harsh punishments became a feature of many of the schools, especially the schools for boys. Absconding, whether in defiance or desperation, was dealt with severely. Although overcrowded and lacking in basic facilities like heating, some of the schools continued to borrow money to expand, and to take in more children. Many of these children were the very young and relatively innocent that almost everyone agreed were not fit subjects for the schools. As David Barclay of the Malone reformatory told the members of the commission established to investigate the reformatory and industrial schools, 'every institution dependent upon the Capitation grant must endeavour to keep up its numbers'.[3]

The Aberdare Commission came to Ireland in early 1883 as part of a wider investigation into reformatory and industrial schools. Lord Aberdare remarked that without the very young and comparatively innocent children in Irish reformatories they would have 'very little ... to do'.[4] Legislation to facilitate the opening of industrial schools was passed in 1868, and by the 1880s the Irish industrial school system had grown beyond all expectation and there were six times as many children in them as in the reformatories. Because the numbers being sent to them were so high, their managers were in a position to refuse admission to the very young criminal children that the Industrial Schools Act of 1868 provided for. The commission failed these young and vulnerable children by not censuring the managers who refused to admit them to their industrial schools, and by not making stronger recommendations for a system to provide for them. While the inspectors who visited the reformatories agreed that smaller schools, like Ballinasloe, were more successful, most closed. A dramatic decline in the number of child criminals meant that, by 1908, half of Irish reformatories had closed.

Despite the fact that two new types of institution existed where criminal children could be incarcerated in the period covered by this study, many juvenile offenders continued to be imprisoned by the courts. Some judges and magistrates tried to find the means to avoid sentencing children to reformatories, especially the young and first offenders, and many served sentences in local gaols instead. For many children, a short sentence of days or weeks in these gaols may have been a better alternative to five years in a remote institution separated from their families and communities. These gaols, while not ideal for children, were at least subject to rigorous inspection. Many reformatory managers resisted outside interference, and a relative lack of external support and inspection meant that they became closed institutions. By the late nineteenth century, however, there was a growing acceptance that the incarceration of children should be avoided whenever possible, and a number of measures, culminating in the Children Act of 1908, were introduced to remove the very young and first offenders from both gaols and reformatories. In Britain, Winston Churchill said that the act 'practically destroyed the statistics on juvenile commitments'.[5] New measures such as probation were introduced, and by 1912 only five children were imprisoned in Ireland.[6]

This study has relied heavily on official reports and on the words of adults who made decisions on how criminal children should be treated. While every effort has been made to include the voices of children, the young offenders who are the subject of this book are rarely heard in the contemporary sources. What we are left with are fragments of their stories as they appear in and disappear from the records of courts, prisons, reformatories and industrial schools.

Notes

[All URL links are valid at time of publication]

INTRODUCTION

1. Manuscripts and Archives Division, The New York Public Library. 'Photographs of Some of the More Serious Offenders', The New York Public Library Digital Collections, 1857, http://digitalcollections.nypl.org/items/510d47dc-95c2-a3d9-e040-e00a18064a99. For more on the background to this album see Peadar Slattery, 'The Uses of Photography in Ireland, 1839–1900', unpublished PhD thesis, Trinity College Dublin, 1992, and Gail Baylis, 'A Few Too Many Photographs? Indexing digital histories', *History of Photography*, vol. 38, no. 1, 2014, pp. 3–20.

2. *Directors of Convict Prisons in Ireland, Annual Report*, HC 1857–8 [2376], pp. 43–57.

3. The reports of the inspectors of prisons usually defined children as 'Not exceeding sixteen years' in the second half of the nineteenth century and this designation is used here unless otherwise stated. 'Child criminals' referred to in this work are those children in this age category who have been found guilty of crime.

4. Joseph Robins, *The Lost Children: A study of charity children in Ireland, 1700–1900* (Dublin: Institute of Public Administration, 1980), p. 1.

5. Jane Barnes, *Irish Industrial Schools, 1868–1908: Origins and development* (Dublin: Irish Academic Press, 1989).

6. Eoin O'Sullivan, 'Juvenile Justice and the Regulation of the Poor: "Restored to virtue, to society and to God"', in Ivana Bacik and Michael O'Connell (eds), *Crime and Poverty in Ireland* (Dublin: Round Hall Sweet & Maxwell, 1998), and Bruce Arnold, *The Irish Gulag: How the state betrayed its innocent children* (Dublin: Gill & Macmillan, 2009), pp. 68–91.

7. Mary Raftery and Eoin O'Sullivan, *Suffer the Little Children: The inside story of Ireland's industrial schools* (Dublin: New Island Books, 1999).

8. *Report of the Commission to Inquire into Child Abuse* (2009).

9. Diarmaid Ferriter, 'Suffer Little Children? The historical validity of memoirs of Irish childhood', in Joseph Dunne and James Kelly (eds),

Childhood and Its Discontents: The first Seamus Heaney lectures (Dublin: The Liffey Press, 2002), pp .69–105.

10. Nial Osborough, *Borstal in Ireland: Custodial provision for the young adult offender, 1906–1974* (Dublin: Institute for Public Administration, 1975); Conor Reidy, *Ireland's 'Moral Hospital': The Irish borstal system, 1906–1956* (Dublin: Irish Academic Press, 2009).

11. Ian Miller, 'Constructing "Moral Hospitals": Improving bodies and minds in Irish reformatories and industrial schools, c. 1851–1890', in Anne Mac Lellan and Alice Mauger (eds), *Growing Pains: Childhood illness in Ireland, 1750–1950* (Dublin: Irish Academic Press, 2013), pp. 105–22.

12. Paul Sargent, *Wild Arabs and Savages: A history of juvenile justice in Ireland* (Manchester: Manchester University Press, 2014). The concept of 'coercive confinement' over a number of 'sites of confinement' in Ireland is considered in Ian O'Donnell and Eoin O'Sullivan, '"Coercive Confinement": An idea whose time has come?', *Incarceration: An International Journal of Imprisonment, Detention and Coercive Confinement*, vol. 1, no. 1, 2020, https://journals.sagepub.com/doi/abs/10.1177/2632666320936440.

13. The 'life courses' of 'delinquent, "difficult" and destitute' children in England are examined in Barry Godfrey, Pamela Cox, Heather Shore and Zoe Alker, *Young Criminal Lives: Life courses and life chances from 1850* (Oxford: Oxford Academic, 2017). Emma D. Watkins looks at the life courses of transported juveniles in *Life Courses of Young Convicts Transported to Van Diemen's Land* (London: Bloomsbury Publishing, 2020). The challenge of finding the voices of children from the past is explored in Kristine Moruzi, Nell Musgrove and Carla Pascoe Leahy, *Children's Voices From the Past: New historical and interdisciplinary perspectives* (Cham, Switzerland: Palgrave Macmillan, 2019).

14. Pamela Cox, Robert Shoemaker and Heather Shore, *Victims and Criminal Justice: A history* (Oxford: Oxford Academic, 2023).

15. Earlier developments in juvenile justice are dealt with in Reidy, *Ireland's 'Moral Hospital'* and Sargent, *Wild Arabs and Savages*.

CHAPTER 1: CRIMINAL CHILDREN AFTER THE FAMINE

1. The word 'gaol' was commonly used in the nineteenth century but was gradually replaced by 'jail' or 'prison'.

2. National Archives of Ireland (hereafter NAI), Register of the County Prison, Galway, PRIS 1/21/3.

3. NAI, Registry of Female Convicts, Grangegorman depot, PRIS 1/9/7.

4. Census of Ireland 1851, Part 1, vi, General Report, HC 1856 [2134], p. xv.

5. *Annual Report of the Commissioners for Administering the Laws for the Relief of the Poor in Ireland*, HC 1852 [1530], summary of returns (hereafter *Report of the Poor Law Commissioners*).

6. 10 & 11 Vict., c. 84.

7. Tim Carey, *Mountjoy: The story of a prison* (Cork: The Collins Press, 2000), p. 44. A female convict prison was established in Mountjoy in 1858.

8. For more on what came to be known as the 'Crofton system', see ibid., chapter 4.

9. A child under the age of seven could not be tried for a felony. The principle of 'doli incapax' determined that children between the ages of seven and fourteen had to be shown in a trial to have acted with criminal intent, a provision that was 'frequently forthcoming'; Sir Leon Radzinowicz and Roger Hood, *A History of English Criminal Law and Its Administration from 1750* (London: Stevens & Sons, 1986), vol. 5, p. 133. See also Dermot Walsh, *Juvenile Justice* (Dublin: Thomson Round Hall, 2005), for legal definitions of childhood and a legislative overview of juvenile justice.

10. *Report of the Inspectors-General of Prisons of Ireland* (hereafter *Inspectors-General Report*), HC 1847–8 [952], p. 5.

11. In December 1847, for example, two-year-old Peggy Mealy, three-year-olds Patt Conway and Mary Dowd, four-year-old Denis Dowd and five-year-old Mary Flaherty were all imprisoned on the same day in Galway gaol for 'asking alms' (NAI, Town Gaol of Galway Register, PRIS 1/21/2).

12. Inspectors-general Report, HC 1854–5 [1956], p. xi.

13. Ibid., 1847–8, p. 8. In the nineteenth century the word 'dietary' was used as a noun.

14. Ibid., HC 1850 [1229], p. viii.

15. NAI, Register of the County Prison, Galway, PRIS 1/21/3.

16. Inspectors-general report, HC 1851 [1364], pp. xv, xix.

17. Select Committee on Criminal and Destitute Juveniles, HC 1852 (515), p. 349. The Irish Poor Relief Act of 1838 established a system of welfare based primarily on the workhouse.

18. Inspectors-general report, 1851, p. xv.

19. Ibid., 1851, general report.

20. Ibid., HC 1852–3 [1657], p. 29.

21. Ibid., 1850, pp. ix, x.

22. Ibid., 1852 [1531], p. 46.

23. Ibid., 1851, p. xvi.

24. Ibid.

25. *Report of the Commissioners of National Education*, HC 1853, 1854 [1834] [1835], p. 629.

26. Inspectors-general report, 1852, p. 48.

27. John Mitchel, *Jail Journal* (Dublin: M.H. Gill, 1921), p. 11.

28. Inspectors-general report, 1847–8, p. 103.

29. *Directors of Convict Prisons in Ireland, Annual Report*, HC 1858 [2531], pp. 30–43.

30. *Report of the Inspector of Government Prisons in Ireland*, HC 1852–3 [1634], p. 32.

31. John Lentaigne, 'Address at Meeting for the Inauguration of the Thirty-first Session', *Journal of the Statistical and Social Inquiry Society of Ireland*, vol. VII, part LII, 1877/8, p. 14.

32. According to the websites of Libraries Tasmania (https://libraries.tas.gov.au/) and the Female Convicts Research Centre Inc. (https://femaleconvicts.org.au/), Margaret was granted a conditional pardon in 1856 and freed by servitude in 1860. She married at least three times and was working as a laundress at the time of her last marriage. She died at her daughter's residence in Tasmania in February 1900.

33. See Carey, *Mountjoy*, pp. 34–7 and 60–2. Hamish Maxwell-Stewart has examined 'the evolution of penal transportation in the Anglophone world' in 'Transportation from Britain and Ireland, 1615–1875', in Clare Anderson (ed.), *A Global History of Convicts and Penal Colonies* (London: Bloomsbury Academic, 2018).

34. Select Committee of the House of Lords Appointed to Inquire into the Execution of the Criminal Law, HC 1847 [534].

35. Ibid., pp. 409, 410.

36. Ibid., Appendix, p. 126.

37. Patrick Maume, 'Pennefather, Richard', in James McGuire and James Quinn (eds), *Dictionary of Irish Biography* (Cambridge: Cambridge University Press, 2009), p. 47.

38. Select Committee of the House of Lords, p. 157.

39. Ibid., pp. 3–8.

40. 10 & 11 Vict., c. 82.

41. 11 & 12 Vict., c. 59.

42. Civil registration of births was not introduced until 1864, therefore, it was at the discretion of the court to decide the age of the child.

43. Select Committee of the House of Lords, p. 410.

44. Ragged schools sometimes supplemented free education with food and clothing for the children.

45. Mary Carpenter, *Reformatory Schools for the Children of the Perishing and Dangerous Classes and for Juvenile Offenders* (London: Gilpin, 1851).

46. Julius Carlebach, *Caring for Children in Trouble* (London: Routledge & Kegan Paul, 1970), pp. 46–9, 40.

47. Select Committee on Criminal and Destitute Juveniles, HC 1852–3 [47], pp. 89–140.

48. Ibid., pp. 344–57.

49. Select Committee on Criminal and Destitute Children, HC 1852–3 [674, 674–1], pp. 337–56.

50. Ibid., pp. 357–67.

51. Ibid., pp. 387–97.

52. Ibid., p. iii.

53. For more on the work of the Philanthropic Society see Doreen Muriel Whitten, 'Protection, Prevention, Reformation: A history of the Philanthropic Society, 1788–1848', unpublished PhD thesis, London School of Economics and Political Science, 2001.

54. For more on the British reformatories see Margaret May, 'A Child's Punishment for a Child's Crime: The reformatory and industrial school movement in Britain, c. 1780–1880', unpublished PhD thesis, University of London, 1981.

55. Stephen A. Toth, *Mettray: A history of France's most venerated carceral institution* (Ithaca, NY: Cornell University Press, 2019).

56. 17 & 18 Vict., c. 86.

57. Anon., 'Our Juvenile Criminals: The school-master or the gaoler', *Irish Quarterly Review* (hereafter *IQR*), vol. 4, no. 13, 1854, pp. 1–71.

58. Anon., 'What the Irish Quarterly Review Has Done for Ireland, for Irish History, and for Irish Literature', *IQR*, vol. 3, no. 12, 1853, p. xiii.

59. W.J. Fitzpatrick, *History of the Dublin Catholic Cemeteries* (Dublin: Catholic Cemeteries Committee, 1900).

60. Patrick Joseph Murray, *Reformatory Schools for Ireland: A letter addressed to the Right Hon. Edward Horsman, M.P., chief secretary for Ireland* (Dublin: W.B. Kelly, 1856), p. 30.

61. HC 1856 (11).

62. *Hansard*, 1856, vol. 140, cc. 495–7.

63. For more on the Protestant missions in the west of Ireland, see Miriam Moffitt, *Soupers and Jumpers: The Protestant missions in Connemara, 1848–1937* (Dublin: Nonsuch Publishing, 2008).

64. Ibid., p. 22.

65. Maria Luddy, *Women and Philanthropy in Nineteenth-Century Ireland* (Cambridge: Cambridge University Press, 1995), p. 68.

66. Emmet Larkin, *The Making of the Roman Catholic Church in Ireland, 1850–1860* (Chapel Hill, NC: University of North Carolina Press, 1980), pp. 99–101.

67. Dublin Diocesan Archives, papers of Cardinal Paul Cullen, letters from laity, February to June 1856.

68. *Freeman's Journal*, 11 June 1856.

69. Dublin Diocesan Archives, papers of Cardinal Paul Cullen, letters from laity, February to June 1856.

70. *Freeman's Journal*, 16 February and 18 April 1856.

71. HC 1856 (133).

72. Sargent, *Wild Arabs and Savages*, p. 94.

73. Murray, *Reformatory Schools for Ireland*.

74. See, for example, 'Inhabitants of Kiltohart Parish, County Leitrim', 'Inhabitants of the Parish of Cong, County Mayo', 'Clergymen in the Diocese of Tuam', 'Roman Catholic Inhabitants of the Parish of Ballygunner, County Waterford' (HC 1856, Public Petitions).

75. Peadar Mac Suibhne, *Paul Cullen and His Contemporaries with Their Letters from 1820–1902*, vol. 2 (Naas: Leinster Leader, 1962), p. 218.

76. *Hansard*, 1857, vol. 144, c. 1297.

77. Anon., 'Quarterly Record of the Progress of Reformatory Schools', *IQR*, vol. 7, no. 28 and vol. 8, no. 29, 1858.

78. Ibid.

79. P.J. Murray, *Notes on Reformatories for Ireland, and for Dublin in Particular* (Dublin: W.B. Kelly, 1858).

80. *Annual Reports of the Inspectors-General of Prisons, 1855*, pp. xii, xxx, and 1859 HC [2557], pp. viii, 102.

81. In April 1856 James O'Brien, MP had written to Paul Cullen that 'Mr Deasy' would call to him in person: Diocesan Archives, letters from laity to Paul Cullen, 5 April 1856.

82. *Hansard*, 1858, vol. 149, cc. 1401–5.

83. A Bill to Promote and Regulate Reformatory Schools for Juvenile Offenders in Ireland, HC 1857–8 (50).

84. *Hansard*, 1858, vol. 150, cc. 520–3.

85. *Cork Examiner*, 17 May 1858.

86. A Bill to Promote and Regulate Reformatory Schools for Juvenile Offenders in Ireland, as Amended in Committee, HC 1857–8 (140).

87. *Hansard*, 1858, vol. 151, cc. 1431–6.

88. Ibid., Lords sitting, cc. 1999–2006.

89. 21 & 22 Vict, c. 103.

90. Caitriona Clear, *Nuns in Nineteenth-Century Ireland* (Dublin: Gill & Macmillan, 1987), p. 37. The role of female religious in charitable and philanthropic work in the nineteenth century is also examined in,

for example, Luddy, *Women and Philanthropy in Nineteenth-Century Ireland*, and Sarah Roddy, 'Doing Good? Irish women, Catholicism and charity, 1852–1922', in Jyoti Atwal, Ciara Breathnach and Sarah-Anne Buckley (eds), *Gender and History: Ireland, 1852–1922* (Abingdon: Routledge, 2023).

91. Jacinta Prunty, *The Monasteries, Magdalen Asylums and Reformatory Schools of Our Lady of Charity in Ireland, 1853–1973* (Dublin: The Columba Press, 2017), p. 173.

CHAPTER 2: THE FIRST REFORMATORIES

1. *First Report of the Inspector Appointed to Visit the Reformatory Schools of Ireland* (hereafter *Report of the Inspector*), HC 1862 [2949], pp. 3, 5, 8.

2. Colin Barr, 'The Re-energising of Catholicism, 1790–1880', in James Kelly (ed.), *The Cambridge History of Ireland, 1730–1880*, vol. 3 (Cambridge: Cambridge University Press, 2018), p. 288.

3. Fergus Campbell has written that by 1891 29 per cent of senior Irish civil servants were Catholic: 'Who Ruled Ireland? The Irish administration, 1879–1914', *The Historical Journal*, vol. 50, no. 3, 2007. Ciaran O'Neill has examined the education of the Irish Catholic elite in the nineteenth century in *Catholics of Consequence: Transnational education, social mobility and the Irish Catholic elite, 1850–1900* (Oxford: Oxford University Press, 2014).

4. *Second Report of the Inspector*, HC 1863 [3194], pp. 5, 6, 13.

5. *First Report of the Inspector*, p. 3.

6. In the official reports nuns are often described as 'Mrs'. Murray referred to her as 'Mrs Lockhart'.

7. *Ninth Report of the Inspector*, HC 1871 [c. 461], p. 40.

8. *First Report of the Inspector*, p. 3.

9. *Second Report of the Inspector*, pp. 74, 78.

10. *First Report of the Inspector*, p. 3.

11. *Freeman's Journal*, 19 June 1860.

12. *Irish Times and Daily Advertiser*, 31 December 1860.

13. Rev. Richard Smyth, *Philanthropy, Proselytism and Crime: A review of the Irish reformatory system, with a glance at the*

reformatories of Great Britain, and at Mr Maguire's industrial schools bill (Londonderry, 1861), pp. 30, 31, 38–44, 53, 54.

14. Ibid., p. 68. Emphasis in original.

15. 'Report, St Kevin's Reformatory', *IQR*, vol. 9, no. 34, 1859, p. 6.

16. Smyth, *Philanthropy, Proselytism and Crime*, p. 20.

17. *Second Report of the Inspector*, p. 69.

18. Carey, *Mountjoy*, pp. 85–7.

19. *First Report of the Inspector*, p. 12.

20. E.C. Wines, *The State of Prisons and of Child-Saving Institutions in the Civilized World* (Cambridge: University Press, 1880), p. 237.

21. A Sister of St Louis, *Memoir of the Life of Sister Mary Genevieve Beale* (Dublin: Sealy, Bryers & Walker, 1904).

22. *Second Report of the Inspector*, p. 69.

23. Ibid., pp. 74, 70.

24. *Belfast News-Letter*, 1 May 1862.

25. *Cork Examiner*, 13 July 1860.

26. *Sixth Report of the Inspector*, HC 1867 [3814], pp. 19–21.

27. NAI, Chief Secretary's Office Registered Papers, 1863, 10520.

28. *Freeman's Journal*, 7 October 1864.

29. NAI, Chief Secretary's Office Registered Papers, 1864, 11606 and 11878.

30. *Fifth Report of the Inspector*, HC 1866 [3691], pp. 32–3.

31. NAI, Galway Register of Male Juveniles, PRIS 1/21/08, 1865. Female prisoners were included in this register.

32. Sargent, *Wild Arabs and Savages*, p. 93.

33. Murray, *Reformatory Schools for Ireland*, p. 9.

34. *Ninth Report of the Inspector*, pp. 5, 42.

35. Sargent, *Wild Arabs and Savages*, p. 93.

36. *Second Report of the Inspector*, pp. 10, 27.

37. Ibid., p. 32.

38. Smyth, *Philanthropy, Proselytism and Crime*, p. 60.

39. 'Report, St Kevin's Reformatory', *IQR*, vol. 9, no. 34, 1859, pp. 3–28.

40. *The Irish Times*, 26 May 1859.

41. 'Report, St Kevin's Reformatory', *IQR*, vol. 9, no. 34, 1859, pp. 3–28.

42. *First Report of the Inspector*, pp. 9, 10.

43. *Third and Fourth Reports of the Inspector*, 1865 [3458], p. 14.

44. Smyth, *Philanthropy, Proselytism and Crime*, chapter 7.

45. *Ninth Report of the Inspector*, pp. 42, 43.

46. *Sixth Report of the Inspector*, pp. 19, 24.

47. NAI, Convict Reference Files, 1867, W.6.

48. Reformatories and Industrial Schools Commission, HC 1884 [c. 3876] [c. 3876.1], pp. 585, 586.

49. *Seventh and Eighth Reports of the Inspector*, HC [c. 180], pp. 12, 13, 17.

50. *Ninth Report of the Inspector*, p. 34.

51. *Cork Examiner*, 9 March 1870; *Ninth Report of the Inspector*, pp. 13, 14. Ten years later, John Lentaigne told of the 'strong impression' William's death had had on him when, as inspector of prisons, he investigated the circumstances of his suicide: 'The Treatment and Punishment of Young Offenders', *Journal of the Statistical and Social Inquiry Society of Ireland*, vol. 8, part 63, 1884/5.

52. *Fifth Report of the Inspector*, p. 31.

53. Sargent, *Wild Arabs and Savages*, p. 130.

54. *Second Report of the Inspector*, p. 17.

55. The recorder of Birmingham (M.D. Hill) and his daughter, *Journal of a Third Visit to the Convict-Gaols, Refuges and Reformatories of Dublin and Its Neighbourhood* (London: Longman, Brown & Co., 1865), pp. 10–12.

56. Matthew Potter, *Amazing Lace: A history of the Limerick lace industry* (Limerick: Limerick City and County Council, 2014), p. 34.

57. *First Report of the Inspector*, p. 10.

58. *Ninth Report of the Inspector*, pp. 40, 41, 94, 95.

59. Ibid., pp. 5, 14, 15.

60. Ibid., pp. 14, 15, 94, 95. Industrial profits are included in receipts.

61. This system of surveillance led Michel Foucault to describe the regime at Mettray as 'the disciplinary form at its most extreme' in *Discipline and Punish: The birth of the prison*, trans. Alan Sheridan (New York: Penguin Books, 1991), pp. 293, 294. Bentham designed a circular prison where the prisoners in their cells could be observed at all times from an inspection tower.

62. Sargent, *Wild Arabs and Savages*, p. 126.

63. A seminal work on the subject of 'total institutions' is Erving Goffman's *Asylums: Essays on the social situation of mental patients and other inmates* (New York: Anchor Books, 1961).

64. *Second Report of the Inspector*, pp. 13, 14, 17, 18, 19.

65. *Freeman's Journal*, 10 April 1861.

66. Toth, *Mettray*, pp. 49, 50.

67. 'Quarterly Record of the Progress of Reformatory and Ragged Schools', *IQR*, vol. 8, no. 29, 1858.

68. *Third and Fourth Reports of the Inspector*, p. 51. Conor Curran has noted that 'drill instruction was becoming more commonplace' in reformatory and industrial schools by the early 1880s: 'Physical Education and Games in Ireland's Reformatory and Industrial Schools, 1858–1922', *Sport in History*, 20 January 2025 (online), https://doi.org/10.1080/17460263.2024.2439279.

69. Smyth, *Philanthropy, Proselytism and Crime*, chapter 3.

70. For events leading to controversy in the south Dublin workhouse, see Helen Burke, *The People and the Poor Law in Nineteenth-Century Ireland* (Littlehampton: WEB, 1987), pp. 211–18, and Anna Clark, 'Wild Workhouse Girls and the Liberal Imperial State in Mid-Nineteenth-Century Ireland', *Journal of Social History*, vol. 39, no. 2, 2005.

71. *International Congress on the Prevention and Repression of Crime* (Washington: Government Printing Office, 1872), pp. 208, 209.

72. Ibid., pp. 260–8.

73. Ibid., p. 209.

74. *Fourteenth Report of the Inspector of Reformatory and Industrial Schools of Great Britain*, House of Lords Papers, 1872 [LVII(1)], pp. 4, 157.

75. Reformatories and Industrial Schools Commission, p. 512.

76. *Second Report of the Inspector*, p. 53.

77. NAI, Chief Secretary's Office Registered Papers, 1863, 5395.

78. *First Report of the Inspector*, p. 12.

79. Select Committee on Poor Relief (Ireland) 1861, HC (408) (408–1), p. 187.

80. Rose had been selling matches (and possibly cigars) at the Kingsbridge train terminus when the assault was alleged to have taken place. Although the police were informed, no prosecution of the man was made because the police claimed there were inconsistencies in Rose's evidence and because Rose admitted accepting money and was overheard by a constable to say that she would 'go with any man who would give her money': Minute Books of the Guardians of the South Dublin Union, March 1861, NAI, BG79. Twelve years later Rose was in Grangegorman prison for the offence of being a 'night walker': NAI, PRIS 1/9/64.

81. *Second Report of the Inspector*, pp. 82, 83.

82. Prunty, *The Monasteries, Magdalen Asylums and Reformatory Schools*, p. 187. Refractory behaviour of girls in Australian reformatories is examined in Kerry Wimshurst, 'Control and Resistance: Reformatory school girls in late nineteenth-century South Australia', *Journal of Social History*, vol. 18, no. 2, 1984, pp. 273–87.

83. *Second Report of the Inspector*, pp. 82, 83.

84. Ibid., p. 84.

85. *Freeman's Journal*, 28 July 1864.

86. *Third and Fourth Reports of the Inspector*, pp. 58, 59.

87. *Reformatory School for Female Juvenile Offenders, Spark's Lake, Monaghan; Manager's Report*, 1862.

88. *Fifth Report of the Inspector*, p. 35.

89. *Ninth Report of the Inspector*, p. 8.

90. NAI, Chief Secretary's Office Registered Papers, 1864, 11202 and 11295.

91. *First Report of the Inspector*, p. 9.

92. *Second Report of the Inspector*, p. 70, and *Belfast News-Letter*, 1 May 1862.

93. *Third and Fourth Reports of the Inspector*, p. 43.

94. *Ninth Report of the Inspector*, p. 39.

95. Moira J. Maguire and Séamus Ó Cinnéide, '"A good beating never hurt anyone": The punishment and abuse of children in twentieth century Ireland', *Journal of Social History*, vol. 38, no. 3, 2005.

96. Reformatories and Industrial Schools Commission, p. 744. Punishments will be dealt with in more detail in chapter 4.

97. *Second Report of the Inspector*, pp. 13, 17, 19.

98. Julius Rodenberg, *The Island of the Saints: A pilgrimage through Ireland* (London: Chapman & Hall, 1861), pp. 312–15.

99. Smyth, *Philanthropy, Proselytism and Crime*, pp. 38, 39.

100. *Sixth Report of the Inspector*, p. 20.

101. O'Sullivan (Bacik and O'Connell, eds), in *Crime and Poverty in Ireland*.

102. Royal Commission on the Nature and Extent of Instruction by Institutions in Ireland for Elementary Education, HC 1870 [C. 6-VII], pp. 197–217.

103. *Journal of a Third Visit to the Convict-Gaols*, pp. 16, 17.

104. *Ninth Report of the Inspector*, pp. 38, 39; NAI, Sligo Gaol Register, PRIS 1/34/07, and *Forty-third Report of the Inspectors-General*, HC 1865 [3522], p. 237.

105. *Third and Fourth Reports of the Inspector*, p. 60.

106. *Reformatory School for Female Juvenile Offenders, Spark's Lake, Monaghan; Manager's Report*, 1861, p. 3.

107. Prunty, *The Monasteries, Magdalen Asylums and Reformatory Schools*, p. 187.

108. *Second Report of the Inspector*, p. 79. Prunty has written that Murray 'intercepted' over £172 intended for the reformatory around this time: ibid., p. 185.

109. *Third and Fourth Reports of the Inspector*, p. 55.

110. Ibid., and *Second Report of the Inspector*, p. 81.

111. *Second Report of the Inspector*, p. 80.

112. *Journal of a Third Visit to the Convict-Gaols*, p. 10.

113. *Second Report of the Inspector*, p. 78.

114. *Fifth Report of the Inspector*, p. 30.

115. Tahaney Alghrani, *Wayward Girls in Victorian and Edwardian England: Pathways in and out of juvenile institutions, 1854–1920* (London: Bloomsbury Publishing, 2024), p. 3.

116. *Second Report of the Inspector*, pp. 71–3.

117. *Third and Fourth Reports of the Inspector*, p. 45.

118. *Journal of a Third Visit to the Convict-Gaols*, pp. 5–9.

119. Greg T. Smith, 'Muffled Voices: Recovering children's voices from England's social margins', in Moruzi, Musgrove and Pascoe Leahy, *Children's Voices from the Past*, p. 270.

120. *Sixth Report of the Inspector*, p. 28.

121. Reformatories and Industrial Schools Commission, p. 745, and NAI, Chief Secretary's Office Registered Papers, 1866, 23366.

122. *Fifth Report of the Inspector*, pp. 31, 32.

123. *Second Report of the Inspector*, p. 54.

124. *Eleventh Report of the Inspector*, HC 1873 [c. 858], pp. 12, 30.

125. *Second Report of the Inspector*, p. 43.

126. Reformatories and Industrial Schools Commission, p. 531.

127. *Eleventh Report of the Inspector*, p. 30.

128. *Third and Fourth Reports of the Inspector*, p. 57.

129. *Second Report of the Inspector*, p. 82.

130. *Sixth Report of the Inspector*, p. 28.

131. *Third and Fourth Reports of the Inspector*, pp. 56–7.

132. Resistance by children in Irish institutions in the twentieth century is explored in Sinead Pembroke, 'Acts of Survival and Resistance in Industrial and Reformatory Schools in Ireland in the Twentieth Century', in Fiona McCann (ed.), *The Carceral Network in Ireland: History, agency and resistance* (Cham, Switzerland: Palgrave Macmillan, 2020).

133. Toth, *Mettray*, pp. 102, 103.

134. *Sixth Report of the Inspector*, p. 31.

135. *Spark's Lake Manager's Reports*, 1861 and 1862. Emphasis in original.

136. *Second Report of the Inspector*, p. 54.

137. *Tenth Report of the Inspector*, HC 1872 [c. 671], p. 10. There will be further discussion of absconding and insubordination in chapter 3.

138. Abscondings and other disciplinary problems were not unique to Irish reformatories. One of the earliest and most public outbreaks in the British system occurred at Mount St Bernard's reformatory for Catholic boys in Leicestershire in 1864. The inspector, Sydney Turner, attributed the problems, in part, to 'an eruption of Irish impulse': Radzinowicz and Hood, *History of English Criminal Law*, pp. 193–202. In 1874 Rev. Joseph Ryan left his post in Upton to take over the management of the English school. A short time later a 'mutiny' occurred when over 100 of the 200 inmates escaped: *Cork Examiner*, 2 September 1875 and *The Nation*, 20 November 1875. For more on abscondings from British reformatories see May, 'A Child's Punishment'. For 'discord' and 'resistance' in Mettray see Toth, *Mettray*.

139. *Seventh and Eighth Reports of the Inspector*, pp. 19, 21.

140. *Sixth Report of the Inspector*, p. 24.

141. *Ninth Report of the Inspector*, p. 35.

142. Ibid.

143. *Fifth Report of the Inspector*, p. 35.

144. *Sixth Report of the Inspector*, p. 33.

145. Reformatories and Industrial Schools Commission, pp. 744, 745.

146. Toth, *Mettray*, p. 4.

147. These relapses will be dealt with in further detail in chapter 3.

148. *Ninth Report of the Inspector*, p. 87. The remainder were 'emigrated', 'sent to sea', 'enlisted', 'specially discharged' or 'absconded and not recovered'.

149. *Sixth Report of the Inspector*, p. 29.

150. *Ninth Report of the Inspector*, pp. 33, 43.

151. Smyth, *Philanthropy, Proselytism and Crime*, p. 7.

152. *Journal of a Third Visit to the Convict-Gaols*, p. 10.

153. *Seventh and Eighth Reports of the Inspector*, p. 22.

154. *Hansard*, 1858, vol. 149, c. 1404.

155. *Sixth Report of the Inspector*, p. 21, and seventh and eighth reports, p. 24.

156. Murray died in 1873: *History of the Dublin Catholic Cemeteries*, p. 131.

157. Enda Leaney, 'Lentaigne, John Francis O'Neill', in McGuire and Quinn (eds), *Dictionary of Irish Biography*.

CHAPTER 3: 'UNSTAINED BY CRIMINALITY'? POOR AND CRIMINAL CHILDREN, 1868–80

1. For more on the concept of pre-delinquency and the 'social risk' model of child care in an Irish context see Denis O'Sullivan, 'Social Definition in Child Care in the Irish Republic: Models of the child and child-care intervention', *Economic and Social Review*, vol. 10, no. 3, 1979. For the English context see May, 'A Child's Punishment'.

2. *Annual Report of the Poor Law Commissioners*, HC 1867–8 [4042], p. 120.

3. Select Committee on Poor Relief, pp. 185, 186.

4. Ibid. See also Virginia Crossman, '"Facts notorious to the whole country": The political battle over Irish Poor Law reform in the 1860s', *Transactions of the Royal Historical Society*, vol. 20, 2010.

5. Simon Gallaher, 'Children's Happiness and Unhappiness in the Irish Workhouse Institution, 1850–1914', in Mary Hatfield (ed.), *Happiness in Nineteenth-Century Ireland* (Liverpool: Liverpool University Press, 2021), p. 120.

6. 25 & 26 Vict., c. 83.

7. *Forty-ninth Report of the Inspectors-General*, HC 1871 [c. 359], p. 574. For more on the treatment of children in workhouses, see Virginia Crossman, 'Cribbed, Contained and Confined? The care of children under the Irish Poor Law, 1850–1920', *Éire/Ireland*, vol. 44, nos. 1 & 2, 2009, pp. 37–61.

8. Linde Lunney, 'Hancock, John', in McGuire and Quinn (eds), *Dictionary of Irish Biography*.

9. Some of these categories were later dropped from the judicial statistics, as Hancock admitted that they related to 'matters of suspicion and opinion, and not to actual crimes committed or suspected': Judicial Statistics, HC 1870 [c. 227], p. 9.

10. Judicial Statistics (Ireland), HC 1863, 1864 [3418], p. xiii. For a discussion of the 'criminal classes' in Ireland at this time see Brian Griffin, *Crime and the Criminal Classes in Ireland, 1870–1920* (Cork: Cork University Press, 2024).

11. Ibid.

12. Industrial Schools (Ireland) Bill, HC 1867 (17).

13. Barnes, *Irish Industrial Schools*, p. 38.

14. Ibid., pp. 18, 41.

15. *Hansard*, 1867, vol. 185, cc. 1741–55.

16. Ibid., 1867, vol. 188, c. 117. See also Barnes, *Irish Industrial Schools*, pp. 38–41.

17. 31 Vict., c. 25.

18. Tenth report of the inspector HC 1872 [c. 671], p. 28.

19. *Seventh and Eighth Reports of the Inspector*, pp. 22, 23.

20. *Freeman's Journal*, 24 June 1869.

21. *Ninth Report of the Inspector*, pp. 16, 17, 59, 60.

22. *Galway Vindicator and Connaught Advertiser*, 20 and 27 November 1872, 4 January 1873.

23. *Twelfth Report of the Inspector*, HC 1874 [c. 969], pp. 17, 18.

24. *Galway Vindicator and Connaught Advertiser*, 15 January 1873.

25. Jane O'Brien, '"It gives great relief to my mind": Family involvement at children's committal to the Sister of Mercy run Irish industrial schools, 1868–1936', *Journal of Family History*, vol. 49, no. 2, 2023, https://doi.org/10.1177/03631990231220603.

26. Barnes, *Irish Industrial Schools*, p. 64.

27. NAI, Galway Register of Male Juveniles, PRIS 1/21/08, 1872.

28. *Freeman's Journal*, 28 January 1875.

29. *Ninth Report of the Inspector*, p. 11.

30. *Nenagh Guardian*, 11 October 1873.

31. *Twelfth Report of the Inspector*, pp. 89–91.

32. Barnes, *Irish Industrial Schools*, p. 69.

33. *Nineteenth Report of the Inspector*, HC 1881 [c. 3070], pp. 8, 9.

34. Barnes, *Irish Industrial Schools*, p. 104.

35. *Nineteenth Report of the Inspector*, pp. 160–2.

36. *Galway Express*, 25 January 1873.

37. *Twenty-third Report of the Inspector*, HC 1884–5 [c. 4553], p. 12.

38. Reformatories and Industrial Schools Commission, p. 519.

39. Ibid., pp. 519, 561.

40. Ibid., p. 529.

41. *Ninth Report of the Inspector*, pp. 7, 8.

42. *Ninth and Fourteenth Reports of the Inspector*, HC 1876 [c. 1494], p. 45.

43. Reformatories and Industrial Schools Commission, pp. 525, 516.

44. *Fourteenth Report of the Inspector*, pp. 45, 46.

45. Miller, 'Constructing "Moral Hospitals"', p. 114.

46. *Nineteenth Report of the Inspector*, p. 44.

47. *Fifty-second Report of the Inspectors-General*, HC 1874 [c. 966], p. 437.

48. *Tenth Report of the Inspector*, p. 42.

49. *Thirteenth Report of the Inspector*, HC 1875 [c. 1222], p. 40.

50. *Seventeenth Report of the Inspector*, HC 1878–9 [c. 2453], p. 38.

51. *Eleventh Report of the Inspector*, p. 37.

52. *Thirteenth Report of the Inspector*, p. 43.

53. *Sixteenth Report of the Inspector*, HC 1878 [c. 2151], p. 37.

54. *Nineteenth Report of the Inspector*, p. 47.

55. NAI, Convict Reference File, 1872, 11B.

56. *Tenth Report of the Inspector*, p. 46.

57. *Seventeenth Report of the Inspector*, p. 41.

58. *Cork Examiner*, 14 May 1874. 'Patrick' may have been referring to events in 1867 when the boys saw a 'detached gang of Fenians' on the mountainside, and guns, pikes and swords were found: NAI, Chief Secretary's Office Registered Papers, 1867, 3920.

59. *Freeman's Journal*, 6 January 1872 and 12 January 1872.

60. *Nenagh Guardian*, 22 April 1874.

61. *Fourteenth Report of the Inspector*, p. 39.

62. *Freeman's Journal*, 9 November 1877.

63. F.R. Falkiner, 'Our Habitual Criminals', *Journal of the Statistical and Social Inquiry Society of Ireland*, vol. 8, part 60, 1881/2, pp. 317–18.

64. *First Report of the General Prisons Board* (hereafter GPB), HC 1878–9 [c. 2447], p. 115.

65. *Fifteenth Report of the Inspector*, HC 1877 [c. 1821], p. 37.

66. NAI, Penal Record File, 1885/105.

67. *Sixteenth Report of the Inspector*, p. 38.

68. *Nineteenth Report of the Inspector*, p. 39.

69. *Twentieth Report of the Inspector*, HC 1882 [c. 3372], p. 44.

70. Fiachra Byrne and Catherine Cox write of 'the gradual recognition in the 1950s and 1960s ... of the necessity to cater for the emotional and psychological needs of offending and non-offending juveniles in residential care settings ...' in '"Straightening crooked souls": Psychology and children in custody in 1950s and 1960s Ireland', in Lynsey Black, Louise Brangan and Deirdre Healy (eds), *Histories of Punishment and Social Control in Ireland: Perspectives from a periphery* (Leeds: Emerald Publishing Limited, 2022).

71. *Freeman's Journal*, 18 February 1871, 10 March 1879.

72. *Munster Express*, 17 May 1873.

73. *Kerry Evening Post*, 25 August 1875.

74. *Leinster Express*, 17 June 1876.

75. Foucault wrote that 'the entire parapenal institution, which is created in order not to be a prison, culminates in the cell': *Discipline and Punish*, p. 294.

76. U.R.Q. Henriques, 'The Rise and Decline of the Separate System of Prison Discipline', *Past and Present*, no. 54, 1972.

77. Thomas J. Clarke, *Glimpses of an Irish Felon's Prison Life* (Dublin: Maunsel & Roberts, 1922), p. 5.

78. NAI, Penal Record File, 1885/85.

79. *Eighteenth Report of the Inspector*, HC 1880 [c. 2692], pp. 35, 36, 41.

80. *Twenty-fourth Report of the Inspector of Reformatory and Industrial Schools of Great Britain*, HC 1881 [c. 3004], pp. 256, 257.

81. *Nineteenth Report of the Inspector*, p. 117.

82. In 1878–9 there were 991 Catholic children in prison, and 126 Protestant and Presbyterian children: first report of the GPB, pp. 66, 67.

83. Prunty, *The Monasteries, Magdalen Asylums and Reformatories*, pp. 192–5.

84. *Nineteenth Report of the Inspector*, p. 40.

85. NAI, Convict Reference File, 1871, 14F.

86. *Tenth Report of the Inspector*, pp. 44, 45.

87. *Thirteenth Report of the Inspector*, p. 41.

88. *Fifteenth Report of the Inspector*, p. 36.

89. *Sixteenth Report of the Inspector*, pp. 36, 37.

90. *Ninth Report of the Inspector*, p. 40.

91. *Tenth Report of the Inspector*, p. 43.

92. *Twelfth Report of the Inspector*, p. 15. This situation would change with the enactment of 44 & 45 Vict. c. 29 which provided for grand juries and town councils to contribute towards building costs or purchase of land for reformatories.

93. *Twelfth Report of the Inspector*, p. 41.

94. *Eighteenth Report of the Inspector*, p. 42.

95. *Nineteenth Report of the Inspector*, pp. 45, 46.

96. *Thirteenth Report of the Inspector*, p. 37.

97. *Belfast News-Letter*, 8 November 1878.

98. *Fifteenth Report of the Inspector*, p. 32.

99. *Nineteenth Report of the Inspector*, p. 42.

100. *Ninth Report of the Inspector*, pp. 38, 39.

101. *Eleventh Report of the Inspector*, p. 33.

102. *Sixteenth Report of the Inspector*, p. 33.

103. *Tenth Report of the Inspector*, p. 40.

104. *Eighteenth Report of the Inspector*, p. 40.

105. *Seventeenth Report of the Inspector*, p. 37.

106. *Cork Examiner*, 27 and 28 August 1872.

107. Reformatories and Industrial Schools Commission, p. 528.

108. *Freeman's Journal*, 18 October 1875.

109. Ibid., 18 August 1877.

110. Mary was about to be sent to a reformatory when it was discovered that she was pregnant. The *Freeman's Journal* called for the prosecution of men who made girls like Mary, who was fifteen, pregnant: ibid., 8 and 9 August 1872. By 16 August, the paper was able to report that her seducer had been discovered and 'a promise of an early marriage has been given'.

111. Reformatories and Industrial Schools Commission, pp. lii, liii.

112. Managers reported that 14.4 per cent of boys and 4.6 per cent of girls had been reconvicted: *Nineteenth Report of the Inspector*, pp. 30, 11.

113. *Forty-ninth Report of the Inspectors-General*, and *Eighteenth Report of the Inspector of Reformatory and Industrial Schools*.

114. *Forty-ninth Report of the Inspectors-General*; *Fifty-fourth Report of the Inspectors-General* (HC 1876 [c. 1497]).

115. The inspectors-general office was replaced by the General Prisons Board (GPB) in 1877.

116. *Fiftieth Report of the Inspectors-General*, HC 1872 [c. 535], pp. 228, 568.

117. *Forty-eighth Report of the Inspectors-General*, HC 1870 [c. 173], pp. 232, 321, 323.

118. *Thirtieth Report of the Inspectors-General*, p. 46.

119. *Forty-ninth Report of the Inspectors-General*, pp. x, 14, 557.

120. *Fiftieth Report of the Inspectors-General*, p. 556.

121. *Fifty-first Report of the Inspectors-General*, HC 1873 [c. 837], p. 580.

122. *Forty-ninth Report of the Inspectors-General*, p. 96.

123. Reformatories and Industrial Schools Commission, p. 584.

124. Both these categories refer to prisoners tried at quarter sessions and assizes.

125. Data extracted from the *Thirty-third and Forty-Eighth Reports of the Inspectors-General of Prisons*.

126. Criminal and Judicial Statistics, Ireland, HC 1868–9 [4203], p. 9.

127. *Forty-seventh Report of the Inspectors-General*, HC 1868–9 [4205], p. 44.

128. *Thirty-third Report of the Inspectors-General*, p. xi.

129. Radzinowicz and Hood, *History of English Criminal Law*, p. 623. For more on the difficulties associated with criminal statistics, see V.A.C. Gatrell and T.B. Hadden, 'Criminal Statistics and Their Interpretation', in E.A. Wrigley (ed.), *Nineteenth-Century Society: Essays in the use of quantitative methods for the study of social data* (Cambridge: Cambridge University Press, 1972), David Philips, *Crime and Authority in Victorian England: The Black Country 1835–1860* (London: Croom Helm, 1977) and Griffin, *Crime and the Criminal Classes*.

130. NAI, Grangegorman (PRIS 1/9/64) and Galway Registers of Male Juveniles, 1870 to 1874. Both contain details of female as well as male juveniles.

131. *Freeman's Journal*, 17 July 1873.

132. *Kerry Sentinel*, 25 July 1879.

133. *Nenagh Guardian*, 29 May 1875.

134. Grangegorman register of male juveniles.

135. *Cork Examiner*, 28 February 1873 and 26 January 1876.

136. Galway Register of Male Juveniles, 1867; *Galway Express*, 13 April and 3 August 1867.

137. Elaine Farrell, *'A most diabolical deed': Infanticide and Irish society, 1850–1900* (Manchester: Manchester University Press, 2013).

138. Catherine was released early on licence and sailed for New York in August 1888 (NAI, penal record file 1888/95); *Irish Times*, 18 April, 16 July and 13 December 1881. Elaine Farrell looks in more detail at the Lavelle case in *Women, Crime and Punishment in Ireland: Life in the nineteenth-century convict prison* (Cambridge: Cambridge University Press, 2020).

139. *Freeman's Journal*, 19 and 21 August 1885.

140. *Cork Examiner*, 20 March 1878.

141. Ibid., 2 August 1873.

142. *Freeman's Journal*, 11 November 1873.

143. *Fifty-fourth Report of the Inspectors-General*, HC 1876 [c. 1497-1], pp. 57-70.

144. *Ballinrobe Chronicle*, 13 July 1872.

145. Geraldine Curtin, *The Women of Galway Jail* (Galway: Arlen House, 2001), pp. 83, 84.

146. *Leinster Express*, 25 December 1875.

147. Griffin, *Crime and the Criminal Classes*, pp. 107, 108.

148. *Roscommon Journal and Western Reporter*, 29 August 1863.

149. *Third Report of the GPB*, HC 1880-1 [c. 3067], p. 53.

150. Reformatories and Industrial Schools Commission, pp. 500, 518, 547.

CHAPTER 4: SAVING CHILDREN FROM 'MORAL RUIN': 1880-1908

1. Crossman, 'Cribbed, Contained and Confined?', pp. 37-8.

2. Royal Commission on the Administration of Prisons in Ireland, HC 1884-5 [c. 4233] [c. 4233-1], p. 463.

3. *Galway Vindicator*, 15 March and *Galway Express*, 18 March 1854.

4. *Fifty-third Report of the Inspectors-General*, HC 1875 [c. 1256], p. 326.

5. *Sixth Report of the GPB*, HC 1884 [c. 4158], p. 57.

6. *Hansard*, 1884, vol. 286, cc. 980-6, cc. 1597-8; 1882, vol. 266, cc. 1837. Even the Society for the Prevention of Cruelty to Children in Britain supported whipping of children as an alternative to imprisonment: Radzinowicz and Hood, *History of English Criminal Law*, pp. 711-19.

7. 47 & 48 Vict., c. 19. For legal interpretation of the act and subsequent relevant legislation, see Walsh, *Juvenile Justice*, pp. 8-11.

8. 47 & 48 Vict., ch. 19.

9. *Eighth Report of the GPB*, HC 1886 [c. 4817], p. 78.

10. Radzinowicz and Hood, *History of English Criminal Law*, pp. 212, 625, 626.

11. *Freeman's Journal*, 22 September 1875.

12. Radzinowicz and Hood, *History of English Criminal Law*, p. 184.

13. 50 & 51 Vict., c. 25.

14. *Fourteenth Report of the GPB*, HC 1892 [c. 6789], pp. 11–13.

15. NAI, General Register, Clonmel Gaol, 1891, PRIS 1/7/12.

16. 1 Edw. 7, c. 20.

17. *Irish Independent*, 3 April 1906.

18. *Kerry Weekly Reporter*, 1 February 1902.

19. *Fermanagh Herald*, 10 March 1906.

20. 7 Edw. 7, c. 17.

21. Thomas Molony, 'The Probation of Offenders', *Journal of the Statistical and Social Inquiry Society of Ireland*, vol. 14, no. 4, 1925, pp. 181–96, and Gerry McNally, 'Probation in Ireland: A brief history of the early years', *Irish Probation Journal*, vol. 4, no. 1, 2007. Miss Gargan is sometimes referred to as 'Dargan'.

22. Sargent, *Wild Arabs and Savages*, p. 100.

23. Ibid., p. 17.

24. 8 Edw. 7, c. 67.

25. *Hansard*, 1908, vol. 183, cc. 1436.

26. Sargent has written that, despite this and subsequent measures, 'a separate court was only ever established in Dublin ... Outside Dublin, the Children Court continued to sit in the same room as the regular District Court': *Wild Arabs and Savages*, p. 46.

27. *Freeman's Journal*, 13 April 1904 and 12 September 1905, and *Irish Daily Independent*, 6 October 1904. The first court for children in England was established in Birmingham in April 1905: Radzinowicz and Hood, *History of English Criminal Law*, pp. 630, 631.

28. Ibid., pp. 630–3.

29. Royal Commission on the Administration of Prisons, p. 280.

30. Departmental Committee on Prisons, HC 1895 [c. 7702].

31. A plank bed was a wooden plank without bedding.

32. *Nineteenth Report of the GPB*, HC 1896–7 [c. 8589], pp. 7, 19, 20.

33. *Twenty-second Report of the GPB*, HC 1900 [cd. 293], p. 12.

34. Oscar Wilde, *Children in Prison and Other Cruelties of Prison Life* (London: Murdoch & Co., 1898).

35. *Evening Herald*, 10 June 1897.

36. *Twenty-eighth Report of the GPB*, HC 1905–6 [cd. 3103], pp. vii, viii.

37. *Thirtieth Report of the GPB*, HC 1908 [cd. 4253], pp. vii, viii.

38. *Thirty-fourth Report of the GPB*, HC 1912–13 [cd. 6365], p. vii. Section 131 of the Children Act defined 'a child' as under the age of fourteen years, and a 'young person' as 'fourteen years of age or upwards and under the age of sixteen years'.

39. 62 & 63 Vict., c. 12.

40. *Irish Times*, 12 May 1900.

41. Radzinowicz and Hood, *History of English Criminal Law*, pp. 221, 222.

42. *Twenty-first Report of the Inspector of Reformatory and Industrial Schools*, HC 1883 [c. 3806], p. 29.

43. Cited in Prunty, *The Monasteries, Magdalen Asylums and Reformatory Schools*, p. 196.

44. Reformatories and Industrial Schools Commission, p. iii.

45. Ibid., pp. 477–83.

46. Patrick M. Geoghegan, 'Falkiner, Sir Frederick Richard', in McGuire and Quinn (eds), *Dictionary of Irish Biography*.

47. Reformatories and Industrial Schools Commission, p. 536.

48. Ibid., pp. 534–44.

49. Ibid., Appendix B 11.

50. 25 Vict., c. 18.

51. Reformatories and Industrial Schools Commission, pp. 508–26.

52. Susan Magarey has examined how the perception of juvenile crime changed, in 'The Invention of Juvenile Delinquency in Early Nineteenth-Century England', *Labour History*, no. 34, 1978.

53. Reformatories and Industrial Schools Commission, p. lxxii.

54. Ibid., p. lvi. Lentaigne challenged this figure by telling the commissioners that many of these committals were of recidivists, and that 373 individual males and forty-eight females accounted for this number.

55. Ibid., pp. lii–lxxii.

56. *Twenty-fourth Report of the Inspector*, HC 1886 [c. 4814], p. 21.

57. *Freeman's Journal*, 16 November 1886.

58. *Twenty-seventh Report of the Inspector*, HC 1889 [c. 5858], p. 31.

59. Ibid., pp. 12, 42.

60. Barnes, *Industrial Schools*, p. 70.

61. *Twenty-eighth Report of the Inspector*, HC 1890 [c. 6168], p. 26.

62. *Thirty-second Report of the Inspector*, HC 1894 [c. 7467], pp. 4–7.

63. *Anglo-Celt*, 11 January 1908.

64. *Fortieth Report of the Inspector*, HC 1902 [cd. 1310], p. 7.

65. *Anglo-Celt*, 14 March 1908.

66. *Thirty-fourth Report of the Inspector*, HC 1896 [c. 8173], p. 4.

67. *Cork Examiner*, 19 August 1903.

68. For more on the Irish borstal system see Osborough, *Borstal in Ireland* and Reidy, *Ireland's 'Moral Hospital'*.

69. 55 & 56 Vict., c. 42.

70. Census of Ireland 1901, HC 1902 [cd. 1190], p. 61.

71. 35 & 36 Vict., c. 38, 60 & 61 Vict., c. 57 and 52 & 53 Vict., c. 44. For more on the Infant Life Protection Acts see Robins, *The Lost Children*, p. 307, and for the issue of 'baby farming' in an Irish context see Ciara Breathnach, 'Infant Life Protection and Medico-Legal Literacy in Early Twentieth-Century Dublin', *Women's History Review*, vol. 26, no. 6, 2017.

72. Sarah-Anne Buckley, *The Cruelty Man: Child welfare, the NSPCC and the state in Ireland, 1889–1956* (Manchester: Manchester University Press, 2013), p. 47.

73. Street-Trading Children Committee (Ireland), HC 1902 [cd. 1144]. See also Gillian McIntosh, 'Children, Street Trading and the Representation of Public Space in Edwardian Ireland', in Maria Luddy and James M. Smith (eds), *Children, Childhood and Irish Society, 1500 to the Present* (Dublin: Four Courts Press, 2014).

74. 3 Edw. 7, c. 45.

75. *Cork Examiner*, 3 November 1903.

76. *Irish Independent*, 6 October 1905.

77. *Thirty-eighth Report of the Inspector*, HC 1900 [cd. 345], p. 38.

78. Reformatories and Industrial Schools Commission, p. 587.

79. *Anglo-Celt*, 11 January 1908; *Nenagh Guardian*, 11 March 1908.

80. *Twenty-seventh Report of the Inspector*, p. 22.

81. *Freeman's Journal*, 30 July 1908.

82. Reformatories and Industrial Schools Commission, p. 587.

83. For more on the work of the Clonmel Discharged Prisoners' Aid Society, later the Borstal Association of Ireland, see Reidy, *Ireland's 'Moral Hospital'*, chapter 8.

84. *Twenty-eighth Report of the GPB*, HC 1906 [cd. 3103], p. 136. Elaine Farrell has examined the assistance given to female convicts to emigrate in '"The salvation of them": Emigration to North America from the nineteenth-century Irish women's convict prison', *Women's History Review*, vol. 25, no. 4, 2016.

85. *Forty-seventh Report of the Inspector*, HC 1909 [cd. 4852], p. 5.

86. Children Act, sections 68–70.

87. *Forty-seventh Report of the Inspector*, pp. 21, 6.

88. Walsh, *Juvenile Justice*, p. 2.

89. Sargent, *Wild Arabs and Savages*, p. 2.

CONCLUSION

1. Carlebach, *Caring for Children*, p. 54.

2. Caitriona Clear, *Social Change and Everyday Life in Ireland, 1850–1922* (Manchester: Manchester University Press, 2007), p. 121.

3. Reformatories and Industrial Schools Commission, p. 477.

4. Ibid., p. 479.

5. Radzinowicz and Hood, *History of English Criminal Law*, p. 629.

6. For developments in youth justice in Ireland in the twentieth century see Sargent, *Wild Arabs and Savages* and Walsh, *Juvenile Justice*.

Bibliography

PRIMARY SOURCES

National Archives of Ireland

Register of the County Prison, Galway, PRIS 1/21/2, 1/21/3

Register of Female Convicts, Grangegorman Depot, PRIS 1/9/7, 1/9/40, 1/9/64

Town Gaol of Galway Register, PRIS 1/21/2

Galway Register of Male Juveniles, PRIS 1/21/08

Sligo Gaol Register, PRIS 1/34/07

General Register, Clonmel Gaol, PRIS 1/7/12

Chief Secretary's Office Registered Papers, 1863, 10520

———, 1863, 5395

———, 1864, 11202, 11295, 11606 and 11878

———, 1866, 23366

———, 1867, 3920

Convict Reference File, 1867, W. 6

———, 1872, 11B

———, 1871, 14F

Penal Record File, 1885/85

———, 1885/105

———, 1888/95

Minute Books of the Guardians of the South Dublin Union, March 1861, BG79

Dublin Diocesan Archives

Papers of Cardinal Paul Cullen, Letters from Laity, February to June 1856

Parliamentary debates, papers and legislation

Hansard, 1856, vol. 140, cc. 495–7

———, 1857, vol. 144, c. 1297

———, 1858, vol. 149, cc. 1401–5

———, 1858, vol. 150, cc. 520–3

———, 1858, vol. 151, cc. 1431–6, cc. 1999–2001

———, 1867, vol. 185, cc. 1741–55

———, 1867, vol. 188, cc. 117

———, 1882, vol. 266, cc. 1837

———, 1884, vol. 286, cc. 980–6, cc. 1597–8

———, 1908, vol. 183, cc. 1436

Select Committee of the House of Lords Appointed to Inquire into the Execution of the Criminal Law, HC 1847 [534] vii, 5

Census of Ireland, 1851, Part 1, General Report, HC 1856 [2134] xxxi, 1

——— 1901, HC 1902 [cd. 1190] cxxix, 1

Select Committee on Criminal and Destitute Juveniles, HC 1852 [515], 1852 [47] vii, 1

Select Committee on Criminal and Destitute Children, HC 1852–3 [674, 674-1] xxiii, 1, 567

Annual Report of the Commissioners for Administering the Laws for the Relief of the Poor in Ireland, HC 1852 [1530] xxiii, 155

———, HC 1868 [4042] xxxiii, 413

Select Committee on Poor Relief (Ireland) 1861, HC (408) (408-1) x.1, 647

Report of the Commissioners of National Education, HC 1853, 1854 [1834] 1835

Report of the Inspector of Government Prisons in Ireland, HC 1852–3 [1634] liii, 277

Directors of Convict Prisons in Ireland, Annual Report, HC 1857–8 [2376] xxx, 389

———, HC 1858 [2531] xiii, 11, 103

Report of the Inspectors-General of Prisons of Ireland, HC 1847–8 [952] xxxiv, 253

———, HC 1850 [1229] xxix, 305

———, HC 1851 [1364] xxviii, 357

———, HC 1852 [1531] xxv, 1

———, HC 1852–3 [1657] liii, 1

———, HC 1854–5 [1956] xxvi, 307

———, HC 1856 [2113] xxxiv, 165

———, HC 1857-58 [2394] xxx.1

———, HC 1860 [2691] xxxvi, 191

———, HC 1862 [3020] xxvi.1

———, HC 1865 [3522] xxiv, 1

———, HC 1868–9 [4205] xxix, 221

———, HC 1870 [c. 173] xxxvii, 233

———, HC 1871 [c. 359] xxx, 1

———, HC 1872 [c. 535] xxxii, 1

———, HC 1873 [c. 837] xxxiii, 1

———, HC 1874 [c. 966] xxix, 757

———, HC 1875 [c. 1256] xxxviii, 1

———, HC 1876 [c. 1497], [1479-1] xxxvi, 1

Report of the General Prisons Board, HC 1878–9 [c. 2447] xxxiv, 353

———, HC 1880–1 [c. 3067] li, 665

———, HC 1884 [c. 4158] xlii, 705

———, HC 1886 [c. 4817] xxxv, 281

———, HC 1892 [c. 6789] xlii, 245

———, HC 1896–7 [c. 8589] xl, 545

———, HC 1900 [cd. 293] xli, 577

———, HC 1905–6 [cd. 3103] li, 45

———, HC 1906 [cd. 3103] li, 45

———, HC 1908 [cd. 4253] lii, 861

———, HC 1912–13 [cd. 6365] xliii, 705

Report of the Inspector Appointed to Visit the Reformatory Schools of Ireland, HC 1862 [2949] xxvi, 651

———, HC 1863 [3194] xxiv, 623

———, HC 1865 [3458] xxv, 569

———, HC 1866 [3691] xxxviii, 545

———, HC 1867 [3814] xxxvi, 819

———, HC 1870 [c. 180] xxxvi, 789

Report of the Inspector Appointed to Visit the Reformatory and Industrial Schools of Ireland, HC 1871 [c. 461] xxviii, 927

———, HC 1872 [c. 671] xxx, 661

———, HC 1873 [c. 858] xxxi, 739

———, HC 1874 [c. 969] xxviii, 771

———, HC 1875 [c. 1222] xxxvi, 795

———, HC 1876 [c. 1494] xxxiv, 777

———, HC 1877 [c. 1821] xlii, 783

———, HC 1878 [c. 2151] xlii, 601

———, HC 1878–9 [c. 2453] xxxvi, 355

———, HC 1880 [c. 2692] xxxvii, 373

———, HC 1881 [c. 3070] liii, 389

———, HC 1882 [c. 3372] xxxv, 397

———, HC 1883 [c. 3806] xxxiv, 421

———, HC 1884–5 [c. 4553] xxxix, 775

———, HC 1886 [c. 4814] xxxvi, 469

———, HC 1889 [c. 5858] xlii, 517

———, HC 1890 [c. 6168] xxxviii, pt. 473

———, HC 1894 [c. 7467] xlv, Pt. I. 495

———, HC 1896 [c. 8173] xlv, 661

———, HC 1900 [cd. 345] xliii, 729

———, HC 1902 [cd. 1310] xlviii, 673

———, HC 1909 [cd. 4852] xlvi, 731

Report of the Inspector of Reformatory and Industrial Schools of Great Britain, 1872, HL [LVII(1)]

———, HC 1881 [c. 3004] lx.1

Judicial Statistics (Ireland), HC 1863, 1864 [3418] lvii, 653

———, HC 1868–9 [4203] lviii, 737

———, HC 1870 [c. 227] lxiii, 753

Reformatories and Industrial Schools Commission, HC 1884 [c. 3876] [c. 3876.1] xlv.1, 89

Royal Commission on the Administration of Prisons in Ireland, HC 1884–5 [c. 4233] [c. 4233-1] xxxviii.1, 259

Departmental Committee on Prisons, HC 1895 [c. 7702] lvi.1, 55

Commission on the Nature and Extent of Instruction by Institutions in Ireland for Elementary Education, HC 1870 [C. 6-VI] xlix.1

Street-Trading Children Committee (Ireland), HC 1902 [cd. 1144] xlix, 209

Report of the Commission to Inquire into Child Abuse (2009)

HC 1856, *Public Petitions*

Bill for the Better Care and Reformation of Juvenile Offenders in Ireland, 1856 (11)

Bill for the Better Care and Reformation of Juvenile Offenders in Ireland (Amended), 1856 (133)

A Bill to Promote and Regulate Reformatory Schools for Juvenile Offenders in Ireland, HC 1857–8 (50)

———, as Amended by Committee, HC 1857–8 (140)
Industrial Schools (Ireland) Bill, HC 1867 (17)

Newspapers

Anglo-Celt

Ballinrobe Chronicle

Belfast News-Letter

Cork Examiner

Derry People

Evening Herald

Fermanagh Herald

Freeman's Journal

Galway Express

Galway Vindicator and Connaught Advertiser

Irish Daily Independent

Irish Independent

Irish Times

Irish Times and Daily Advertiser

Kerry Evening Post

Kerry Sentinel

Kerry Weekly Reporter

Leinster Express

Munster Express

Nenagh Guardian

Roscommon Journal and Western Reporter

The Nation

Westmeath Examiner

CONTEMPORARY SOURCES

Anon, 'What the Irish Quarterly Review Has Done for Ireland, for Irish History, and for Irish Literature', *Irish Quarterly Review*, vol. 3, no. 12, 1853, p. xiii

———, 'Our Juvenile Criminals: The school-master or the gaoler', *Irish Quarterly Review*, vol. 4, no. 13, 1854, pp. 1–71

———, 'Quarterly Record of the Progress of Reformatory Schools', *Irish Quarterly Review*, vol. 7, no. 28, 1858

———, 'Quarterly Record of the Progress of Reformatory and Ragged Schools', *Irish Quarterly Review*, vol. 8, no. 29, 1858

———, 'Report. St Kevin's Reformatory', *Irish Quarterly Review*, vol. 9, no. 34, 1859

A Sister of St Louis, *Memoir of the Life of Sister Mary Genevieve Beale* (Dublin: Sealy, Bryers & Walker, 1904)

Carpenter, Mary, *Reformatory School for the Children of the Perishing and Dangerous Classes and for Juvenile Offenders* (London: Gilpin, 1851)

Falkiner, Frederick, 'Our Habitual Criminals', *Journal of the Statistical and Social Inquiry Society of Ireland*, vol. 8, 1881/2

The Recorder of Birmingham (M.D. Hill) and his daughter, *Journal of a Third Visit to the Convict-Gaols, Refuges and Reformatories of Dublin and Its Neighbourhood* (London: Longman, Brown & Co., 1865)

Lentaigne, John, 'The Treatment and Punishment of Young Offenders', *Journal of the Statistical and Social Inquiry Society of Ireland*, vol. 8, part 63, 1884/5

———, 'Address at a Meeting for the Inauguration of the Thirty-first Session', *Journal of the Statistical and Social Inquiry Society of Ireland*, vol. 7, part 52, 1877/8

Murray, Patrick Joseph, *Reformatory Schools for Ireland: A letter addressed to the Right Hon. Edward Horsman, M.P., chief secretary for Ireland* (Dublin: W.B. Kelly, 1856)

———, *Notes on Reformatories for Ireland, and for Dublin in Particular* (Dublin: W.B. Kelly, 1858)

Reformatory School for Female Juvenile Offenders, Spark's Lake, Monaghan; Manager's Report, 1861

Reformatory School for Female Juvenile Offenders, Spark's Lake, Monaghan; Manager's Report, 1862

Rodenberg, Julius, *The Island of the Saints: A pilgrimage through Ireland* (London: Chapman & Hall, 1861)

Smyth, Rev. Richard, *Philanthropy, Proselytism and Crime: A review of the Irish reformatory system, with a glance at the reformatories of Great Britain, and Mr Maguire's industrial school bill* (Londonderry, 1861)

Wines, E.C., *International Congress on the Prevention and Repression of Crime* (Washington: Government Printing Office, 1872)

———, *The State of the Prisons and of Child-Saving Institutions in the Civilised World* (Cambridge: University Press, 1880)

Books and articles

Alghrani, Tahaney, *Wayward Girls in Victorian and Edwardian England: Pathways in and out of juvenile institutions, 1854–1920* (London: Bloomsbury Publishing, 2024)

Anderson, Clare (ed.), *A Global History of Convicts and Penal Colonies* (London: Bloomsbury Academic, 2018)

Arnold, Bruce, *The Irish Gulag: How the state betrayed its innocent children* (Dublin: Gill & Macmillan, 2009)

Barnes, Jane, *Irish Industrial Schools, 1868–1908: Origins and development* (Dublin: Irish Academic Press, 1989)

Barr, Colin, 'The Re-energising of Catholicism, 1790–1880', in James Kelly (ed.), *The Cambridge History of Ireland, 1730–1880*, vol. 3 (Cambridge: Cambridge University Press, 2018)

Baylis, Gail, 'A Few Too Many Photographs? Indexing digital histories', *History of Photography*, vol. 38, no. 1, 2014

Breathnach, Ciara, 'Infant Life Protection and Medico-Legal Literacy in Early Twentieth-Century Dublin', *Women's History Review*, vol. 26, no. 6, 2017

Buckley, Sarah-Anne, *The Cruelty Man: Child welfare, the NSPCC and the state in Ireland, 1889–1956* (Manchester: Manchester University Press, 2013)

Burke, Helen, *The People and the Poor Law in Nineteenth-Century Ireland* (Littlehampton: WEB, 1987)

Byrne, Fiachra and Catherine Cox, '"Straightening Crooked Souls": Psychology and children in custody in 1950s and 1960s Ireland', in Lynsey Black, Louise Brangan and Deirdre Healy (eds), *Histories of Punishment and Social Control in Ireland: Perspectives from a periphery* (Leeds: Emerald Publishing Limited, 2022)

Campbell, Fergus, 'Who Ruled Ireland? The Irish administration, 1879–1914', *The Historical Journal*, vol. 50, no. 3, 2007

Carey, Tim, *Mountjoy: The story of a prison* (Cork: The Collins Press, 2000)

Carlebach, Julius, *Caring for Children in Trouble* (London: Routledge & Kegan Paul, 1970)

Clark, Anna, 'Wild Workhouse Girls and the Liberal Imperial State in Mid-Nineteenth-Century Ireland', *Journal of Social History*, vol. 39, no. 2, 2005

Clarke, Thomas J., *Glimpses of an Irish Felon's Prison Life* (Dublin: Maunsel & Roberts, 1922)

Clear, Catriona, *Nuns in Nineteenth-Century Ireland* (Dublin: Gill & Macmillan, 1987)

———, *Social Change and Everyday Life in Ireland, 1850–1922* (Manchester: Manchester University Press, 2007)

Cox, Pamela, Robert Shoemaker and Heather Shore, *Victims and Criminal Justice: A history* (Oxford: Oxford Academic, 2023)

Crossman, Virginia, 'Cribbed, Contained and Confined? The care of children under the Irish Poor Law, 1850–1920', *Éire/Ireland*, vol. 44, no. 1, 2009

———, '"Facts notorious to the whole country": The political battle over Irish Poor Law reform in the 1860s', *Transactions of the Royal Historical Society*, vol. 20, 2010

Curran, Conor, 'Physical Education and Games in Ireland's Reformatory and Industrial Schools, 1858–1922', *Sport in History*,

20 January 2025 (online), https://doi.org/10.1080/17460263.2024.2439279

Curtin, Geraldine, *The Women of Galway Jail* (Galway: Arlen House, 2001)

Farrell, Elaine, *'A Most Diabolical Deed': Infanticide and Irish society, 1850–1900* (Manchester: Manchester University Press, 2013)

———, '"The salvation of them": Emigration to North America from the nineteenth-century Irish women's convict prison', *Women's History Review*, vol. 25, no. 4, 2016

———, *Women, Crime and Punishment in Ireland: Life in the nineteenth-century convict prison* (Cambridge: Cambridge University Press, 2020)

Ferriter, Diarmaid, 'Suffer Little Children? The historical validity of memoirs of Irish childhood', in Joseph Dunne and James Kelly (eds), *Childhood and Its Discontents: The first Seamus Heaney lectures* (Dublin: Liffey Press, 2002)

Fitzpatrick, William J., *History of the Dublin Catholic Cemeteries* (Dublin: Catholic Cemeteries Committee, 1900)

Foucault, Michel, *Discipline and Punish: The birth of the prison*, trans. Alan Sheridan (London: Penguin Books, 1991)

Gallaher, Simon, 'Children's Happiness and Unhappiness in the Irish Workhouse Institution, 1850–1914', in Mary Hatfield (ed.), *Happiness in Nineteenth-Century Ireland* (Liverpool: Liverpool University Press, 2021)

Gattrell, V.A.C. and T.B. Hadden, 'Criminal Statistics and Their Interpretation' in E.A. Wrigley (ed.), *Nineteenth-Century Society: Essays in the use of quantitative methods for the study of social data* (Cambridge: Cambridge University Press, 1972)

Geoghegan, Patrick M., 'Falkiner, Sir Frederick Richard', in James McGuire and James Quinn (eds), *Dictionary of Irish Biography* (Cambridge: Cambridge University Press, 2009)

Godfrey, Barry S., Pamela Cox, Heather Shore and Zoe Alker, *Young Criminal Lives: Life courses and life chances from 1850* (Oxford: Oxford University Press, 2017)

Goffman, Erving, *Asylums: Essays on the social situation of mental patients and other inmates* (New York: Anchor Books, 1961)

Griffin, Brian, *Crime and the Criminal Classes in Ireland, 1870–1920* (Cork: Cork University Press, 2024)

Henriques, U.R.Q., 'The Rise and Decline of the Separate System of Prison Discipline', *Past and Present*, no. 54, 1972

Larkin, Emmet J., *The Making of the Roman Catholic Church in Ireland, 1850–1860* (Chapel Hill, NC: University of North Carolina Press, 1980)

Leaney, Enda, 'Lentaigne, John Francis O'Neill', in McGuire and Quinn (eds), *Dictionary of Irish Biography*

Luddy, Maria, *Women and Philanthropy in Nineteenth-Century Ireland* (Cambridge: Cambridge University Press, 1995)

Lunney, Linde, 'Hancock, John', in McGuire and Quinn (eds), *Dictionary of Irish Biography*

Mac Suibhne, Peadar, *Paul Cullen and His Contemporaries with Their Letters from 1820–1902*, vol. 2 (Naas: Leinster Leader, 1962)

Magarey, Susan, 'The Invention of Juvenile Delinquency in Early Nineteenth-Century England', *Labour History*, no. 34, 1978

Maguire, Moira J. and Séamus Ó Cinnéide, '"A good beating never hurt anyone": The punishment and abuse of children in twentieth century Ireland', *Journal of Social History*, vol. 38, no. 3, 2005

Maume, Patrick, 'Pennefather, Richard', in McGuire and Quinn (eds), *Dictionary of Irish Biography*

Maxwell-Stewart, Hamish, 'Transportation from Britain and Ireland, 1615–1875', in Clare Anderson (ed.), *A Global History of Convicts and Penal Colonies* (London: Bloomsbury Academic, 2018)

McIntosh, Gillian, 'Children, Street Trading and the Representation of Public Space in Edwardian Ireland', in Maria Luddy and James E. Smith, (eds), *Children, Childhood and Irish Society, 1500 to the Present* (Dublin: Four Courts Press, 2014)

McNally, Gerry, 'Probation in Ireland: A brief history of the early years', *Irish Probation Journal*, vol. 4, no. 1, 2007

Miller, Ian, 'Constructing "Moral Hospitals": Improving bodies and minds in Irish reformatories and industrial schools, c. 1851–1890', in Anne MacLellan and Alice Mauger (eds), *Growing Pains: Childhood illness in Ireland, 1750–1950* (Dublin: Irish Academic Press, 2013)

Mitchel, John, *Jail Journal* (Dublin: M.H. Gill, 1921)

Moffitt, Miriam, *Soupers and Jumpers: The Protestant missions in Connemara, 1848–1937* (Dublin: Nonsuch Publishing, 2008)

Molony, Thomas, 'The Probation of Offenders', *Journal of the Statistical and Social Inquiry Society of Ireland*, vol. 14, no. 4, 1925, pp. 181–96

Moruzi, Kristine, Nell Musgrove and Carla Pascoe Leahy (eds), *Children's Voices from the Past: New historical and interdisciplinary perspectives* (Cham, Switzerland: Palgrave Macmillan, 2019)

O'Brien, Jane, '"It gives great relief to my mind": Family involvement at children's committal to the Sister of Mercy run Irish industrial schools, 1868–1936', *Journal of Family History*, vol. 49, no. 2, 2023, https://doi.org/10.1177/03631990231220603

O'Donnell, Ian and Eoin O'Sullivan, '"Coercive Confinement": An idea whose time has come?', *Incarceration: An international journal of imprisonment, detention and coercive confinement*, vol. 1, no. 1, 2020, https://journals.sagepub.com/doi/abs/10.1177/2632666320936440

O'Neill, Ciaran, *Catholics of Consequence: Transnational education, social mobility and the Irish Catholic elite, 1850–1900* (Oxford: Oxford University Press, 2014)

Osborough, Nial, *Borstal in Ireland: Custodial provision for the young adult offender, 1906–1974* (Dublin: Institute for Public Administration, 1975)

O'Sullivan, Denis, 'Social Definition in Child Care in the Irish Republic: Models of the child and child-care intervention', *Economic and Social Review*, vol. 10, no. 3, 1979

O'Sullivan, Eoin, 'Juvenile Justice and the Regulation of the Poor: "Restored to virtue, to society and to God"', in Ivana Bacik and Michael O'Connell (eds), *Crime and Poverty in Ireland* (Dublin: Round Hall Sweet & Maxwell, 1998)

Pembroke, Sinead, 'Acts of Survival and Resistance in Industrial and Reformatory Schools in Ireland in the Twentieth Century', in Fiona

McCann, *The Carceral Network in Ireland: History, agency and resistance* (Cham, Switzerland: Palgrave Macmillan, 2020)

Philips, David, *Crime and Authority in Victorian England: The Black Country* (London: Croom Helm, 1977)

Potter, Matthew, *Amazing Lace: A history of the Limerick lace industry* (Limerick: Limerick City and County Council, 2014)

Prunty, Jacinta, *The Monasteries, Magdalen Asylums and Reformatory Schools of Our Lady of Charity in Ireland, 1853–1973* (Dublin: The Columba Press, 2017)

Radzinowicz, Sir Leon and Roger Hood, *A History of English Criminal Law and Its Administration from 1750*, vol. 5 (London: Stevens & Sons, 1986)

Raftery, Mary and Eoin O'Sullivan, *Suffer the Little Children: The inside story of Ireland's industrial schools* (Dublin: New Island, 1999)

Reidy, Conor, *Ireland's 'Moral Hospital': The Irish borstal system, 1906–1956* (Dublin: Irish Academic Press, 2009)

Robins, Joseph, *The Lost Children: A study of charity children in Ireland, 1700–1900* (Dublin: Institute of Public Administration, 1980)

Roddy, Sarah, 'Doing Good? Irish women, Catholicism and charity, 1852–1922', in Jyoti Atwal, Ciara Breathnach and Sarah-Anne Buckley (eds), *Gender and History: Ireland, 1852–1922* (Abingdon: Routledge, 2023)

Sargent, Paul, *Wild Arabs and Savages: A history of juvenile justice in Ireland* (Manchester: Manchester University Press, 2014)

Smith, G.T., 'Muffled Voices: Recovering children's voices from England's social margins', in Moruzi, Musgrove and Pascoe Leahy (eds), *Children's Voices from the Past* (Cambridge: Cambridge University Press, 2009)

Walsh, Dermot, *Juvenile Justice* (Dublin: Thomson Round Hall, 2005)

Watkins, Emma D., *Life Courses of Young Convicts Transported to Van Diemen's Land* (London: Bloomsbury Publishing, 2020)

Wimshurst, Kerry, 'Control and Resistance: Reformatory school girls in late nineteenth-century South Australia', *Journal of Social History*, vol. 18, no. 2, 1984

Online Resources

Female Convicts Research Centre Inc., https://femaleconvicts.org.au

Libraries Tasmania, https://libraries.tas.gov.au/

Manuscripts and Archives Division, the New York Public Library, 'Photographs of Some of the More Serious Offenders', the New York Public Library Digital Collections, 1857, https://digitalcollections.nypl.org/items/510d47dc-95c2-a3d9-e040-e00a18064a99

Theses

May, Margaret, 'A Child's Punishment for a Child's Crime: The reformatory and industrial school movement in Britain, *c.* 1780–1880', unpublished PhD thesis, University of London, 1981

Slattery, Peadar, 'The Uses of Photography in Ireland, 1839–1900', unpublished PhD thesis, Trinity College Dublin, 1992

Whitten, Doreen Muriel, 'Protection, Prevention, Reformation: A history of the Philanthropic Society, 1788–1848', unpublished PhD thesis, University of London, 2001

Index

Aberdare, Henry Bruce, Lord, 140–1, 145, 161
Aberdare Commission (1883), 5, 139, 140–7, 152, 160–1
abscondings
  from employment or apprenticeship, 123
  from industrial schools, 90
  from reformatories, 35, 58, 61, 71–2, 74–5, 94–5, 97–9, 109–10, 115–16, 122–3, 143, 160
  from workhouses, 122–3
abuse, 2, 56–7, 137, 139
agricultural labour, 61, 68, 93, 110
Ahern, Peter, 120–1
Alghrani, Tahaney, 68
America, 22, 50, 71, 74, 131, 135, 152
Armagh gaol, 116
Artane industrial school, 89, 90, 91, 110, 147
assault, 94, 111, 119, 148
Australia, 8, 109, 135

Bagwell, John, 32–3
Ball, John, 19–20
Ballinasloe reformatory, 34, 45–6, 62, 65–6, 110, 118, 144, 161
Ballinrobe, 121–2
Bandon, 68, 149
bands, 68, 97
Barclay, David, 61, 140–1, 160
Barnes, Jane, 2, 87, 89, 90, 149
Barry, William, 96–7
Beale, Sr Genevieve, 42–3, 60, 66, 71, 74, 105–8, 149
bee-keeping, 110
begging, 4, 8, 11, 21, 24, 84, 85, 90, 142; *see also* vagrancy

Belfast, 43–4, 51, 61, 63–4, 109, 122, 140–1, 149, 151
Belfast gaol, 52, 135
Belgium, 4, 29, 30–1
Belvedere Crescent reformatory, 30
Bentham, Jeremy, 54
Berwick, Walter, 21, 22, 30, 31
Better Care and Reformation of Youthful Offenders Act, 23–4
Bianconi, Charles, 43
Birr bridewell, 138
Bishop, Henry, 87–8
Blennerhassett, Rowland, 148
borstals, 2, 150, 154
Bourke, Charles, 121
Brady, Margaret, 61
Brazil, 73
bridewells, 8, 135
Bristol, 18, 23
Britain
  borstals, 150
  Children Act, 162
  crime rates, 82–3
  emigration to, 103
  industrial schools, 83, 84, 139–40, 145
  prisons, 23, 102, 136–7
  reformatories, 4, 18–19, 23–4, 30, 55, 58, 68, 104, 131, 139–40, 145, 158
  sentencing practices, 131
  vagrancy, 82–3, 84
Brown, Ellen, 66
buildings
  funding for, 33, 43, 48–9, 92, 108–9
  prison construction, 9
  purpose-built facilities, 44, 49, 75, 104, 108–9
  renovations, 48–9, 92

Index

burglary, 8, 87–8, 102, 122, 133; *see also* stealing
Burke, Mary, 45, 62, 65

Calder Farm school, 55
Carpenter, Mary, 18–19, 23–5, 29, 52, 86, 158, 160
carpentry, 68, 92
Carrick-on-Shannon gaol, 102
Catholic Church, 26–9, 35–6, 46, 83, 158
Catholic Defence Association, 27
Catholicism, 26–9, 34–6, 38–46, 83, 104, 128, 148–9, 158, 159
Chandler, Sarah, 131
chaplains, 15, 16, 18, 39, 113, 128, 135, 136
Children Act, 5, 133–4, 138–9, 149–50, 153–5, 162
children's labour
  income from, 47, 50–4, 75, 107, 108, 109
  in reformatories, 42, 47, 50–4, 61, 63, 65, 68, 75, 92–3, 104, 107–10, 160
Christian Brothers, 29, 30, 89
Churchill, Winston, 162
Clancarty, William Thomas Le Poer Trench, 3rd earl, 34
Clarke, Thomas, 102
Clay, John, 25
Clonmel borstal, 154
Clonmel prison, 14
commissioners of national education, 13, 77, 91, 92
commissions of enquiry *see* government enquiries and reports
Conneely, Denis, 120
Connellan, James Corry, 20–2
Connemara, 26
Connolly, Julia, 58, 74
Conway, Daniel, 90

Cooke, Miss, 39, 109
Cork, 20–1, 30–2, 44–5, 64, 68, 98, 100–1, 103, 120, 140, 145, 151, 153–4
Cork gaol, 21
Cork Street reformatory, 39, 52–3, 67–8, 109, 144, 149
Cormack, Martin, 8, 11
corporal punishment, 8, 16, 17, 62, 114, 123–4, 129–30, 144
Costigan, William, 99
courts
  behaviour of children and families in, 3, 5, 101–2
  lower courts, 17, 117, 129–30, 142–3
  petty sessions courts, 8, 34, 86–8, 99, 123, 130, 133
  sending of children to industrial schools, 5, 85–9, 124, 149–50
  sending of children to reformatories, 23, 33, 44–6, 87–9, 101–2, 111, 124, 148–9
  sentencing practices, 16, 117–18, 130–3, 159, 161
  separate courts for children, 134
  summary trials, 17, 34, 117–18, 129–30
crime rates, 4, 31–2, 76, 145, 146
Crofton, Walter, 9, 38, 42, 49, 53, 54, 86
Cronin, Patrick, 119
Cullen, Paul, 27–8, 35, 38, 40, 42, 46, 57, 80–1, 83
Cushnahan, Teresa, 61, 64

Daily Chronicle, 136
Dalbeth reformatory, 39
D'Arcy, John, 15–16
Davenport Hill, Matthew, 18, 25, 29, 52–3, 64–5, 67, 68, 76
Deasy, Rickard, 32–3, 77

death penalty, 134
deaths
  in prisons, 9, 52
  in reformatories, 93, 95
  suicides, 52, 93
Dee, William, 132
Delaney, Mary, 69, 74–5
Delany, William, 30
Demetz, Frédéric-Auguste, 23, 57
Derry, John, 28, 45
Devereux, Patrick, 111
diet *see* food
discipline
  corporal punishment, 62, 114, 144
  food restrictions, 55, 62
  marks system, 39, 41–2, 54, 61, 62
  mental health impacts, 102–3
  military discipline, 30, 55–6
  in prisons, 17, 54, 113–14
  in reformatories, 4, 30, 39, 41–2, 54–62, 69–70, 94–5, 97–9, 102–3, 105, 143–4, 160
  restraints, 58, 69
  solitary confinement, 62, 94, 102, 144
  solitary working, 55
disease, 9, 12, 13, 95–6
Downes, Nannie, 132–3
drunkenness, 121–2
Dublin
  Aberdare Commission hearings, 140–5
  assaults, 119
  collection of parental contributions, 47
  crime rates, 11–12, 31
  drunkenness, 121
  fundraising meetings, 48
  grand juries, 31, 41
  Magdalene asylums, 35
  police, 12
  poverty, 11–12, 81, 82, 141, 151

prison registers, 118–23
prisons *see* Grangegorman prison; Mountjoy prison; Richmond bridewell
proselytising, 26–8
prostitution, 81, 122
reformatories *see* Cork Street reformatory; Goldenbridge reformatory; High Park reformatory; Rehoboth Place reformatory
separate court for children, 134
stealing, 11–12, 87–8, 105, 118–19
street trading, 151
supervision of discharged children, 100–1
workhouses, 57, 59, 81, 122–3
Dublin Castle, 38, 87, 98
Dublin Catholic Reformatory Committee, 35
Dublin Gazette, 34
Dublin Metropolitan Police, 12, 34, 133; *see also* police
Dublin Statistical Society, 82
Dunlea, John, 118

education
  literacy, 1, 96–7, 150
  literary education, 14, 66, 67, 68, 96–7, 104, 107, 108, 142
  national schools, 26, 29, 66, 107
  in prisons, 1, 13–14, 115–16
  ragged schools, 18–19, 25, 27
  in reformatories, 63, 65–6, 68, 93, 96–7, 104, 107, 108
  and religion, 26–8, 38, 158
  religious education, 19
  schoolmasters, 1, 13–14, 16, 93, 97
  vocational training, 14, 52–3, 92, 104, 107, 108, 136, 141
Education Act, 150
Egan, John, 46

emigration, 22, 50, 59, 71, 73–4, 103, 109, 152, 154
employment, 44, 69, 70–1, 73–4, 100, 105, 109, 123, 152, 154
Employment of Children Act, 151
Ennis gaol, 12, 15–16
Enniskillen, 133
escapes *see* abscondings
exercise, 15, 96, 136

Fagan, John, 148–9, 151
Falkiner, Frederick, 139, 141–3, 159
'family system', 22, 23, 49, 57
Famine *see* Great Famine
Farrell, Elaine, 120
Farrington, Michael, 118
Faulkes, James, 119
Field, John, 25
fines, 17, 123–4, 130
first offenders, 88, 131–3, 141, 143, 154, 161
Fleming, Mary, 105
food
  prisons, 9, 12
  reformatories, 22, 55, 62, 63, 107
  restrictions on as punishment, 55, 62
  workhouses, 9
Fortescue, Chichester, 84
Foster, Michael, 119
foster families, 81, 83
Fox, Lawrence Charles Prideaux, 57, 101
France, 4, 19, 23, 29, 30, 56, 57
Freeman's Journal, 60
funding
  for buildings, 33, 43, 48–9, 92, 108
  from children's labour, 47, 50–4, 75, 107, 108, 109
  fundraising, 40, 43, 44, 48–9
  from grand juries, 34

of industrial schools, 5, 85
local authority funding, 33, 47, 54, 124
parental contributions, 34–5, 47
of reformatories, 4, 19, 23–4, 33–5, 43–4, 47–54, 75–7, 107–9, 140–1, 160
Treasury funding, 23–4, 34, 47, 49, 54, 85, 108, 124
voluntary contributions, 23–4, 47, 53–4
fundraising, 40, 43, 44, 48–9; *see also* voluntary contributions
Furlong, Rev. Moses, 44–5, 50, 51–2, 64

Galvin, Bridget, 128
Galvin, Cornelius, 119
Galway, 8, 12, 19–20, 45–6, 86–7, 118–23
Galway gaol, 8, 12, 114, 118, 120, 128–9, 138
gaols *see* prisons
Gargan, Kathleen, 133
General Prisons Board, 137–8, 147
Germany, 19
Gibson, Edward, 129
Gilbert, J.T., 25
Gladstone Committee (1894), 135
Glasgow, 39, 61
glass-breaking, 11, 21
Glencree reformatory, 40–1, 48–52, 54–8, 68, 75, 95–101, 104, 111, 133, 144, 146, 148, 153
Going, Caleb, 88
Goldenbridge reformatory, 30, 41–2, 58–60, 70–1
good behaviour privileges, 39, 42, 54
government enquiries and reports
  Aberdare Commission (1883), 5, 139, 140–7, 152, 160–1
  Gladstone Committee (1894), 135
  House of Lords Select Committee (1847), 15–17

Royal Commission on the Administration of Prisons (1884–5), 128
Ryan Report (2009), 2
Select Committee on Criminal and Destitute Juveniles (1852–3), 18–23
Select Committee on Poor Relief (1861), 80–1
grand juries, 31, 34, 41
Grangegorman prison, 58, 70, 81, 118, 136
Great Famine, 3, 4, 8, 36, 145
Griffin, Brian, 122

hair cutting, 44, 144
Hammersmith reformatory, 30
Hanna, Thomas, 43, 61
Hannon, Michael, 88
Harcourt, Sir William, 131
hard labour, 13, 16, 21, 61, 99, 119
Haugh, John, 119
Hawthorne, William, 40–1, 64
health
 disease, 9, 12, 13, 95–6
 mental health, 101–2
 in prisons, 9, 12, 13
 in reformatories, 93, 95–6, 107, 110
Healy, Thomas, 87–8
heating, 93, 96, 160
Hicks-Beach, Michael, 140
Higgins, Sarah Anne, 118
Higgins, Thomas, 86
High Park reformatory, 35, 39, 58, 59, 64–7, 69, 74, 104–5, 122, 144, 149
homelessness, 8, 90, 100; *see also* vagrancy
Horsman, Edward, 25, 27, 28–9
House of Lords Select Committee (1847), 15–17
Howard Association, 131
Hue and Cry, 98

industrial schools
 Aberdare Commission enquiry, 5, 139, 140–7, 152, 160–1
 abscondings, 90
 abuse, 2, 139
 in Britain, 83, 84, 139–40, 145
 establishment, 5, 80, 83–7, 161
 funding, 5, 85
 probationary industrial schools, 89, 101, 146, 148
 prosecution of children in their care, 89–90
 refusals of admission, 88–9, 161
Industrial Schools Act, 84–6, 88, 161
Industrial Schools (Ireland) Bill, 83–4
Infant Life Protection Act, 150
infanticide, 120
institutionalisation, 54–5
Irish Daily Independent, 134
Irish Quarterly Review, 24–5, 31, 48
Irish Times, 40, 48

Johnson, Robert, 118, 131

Kavanagh, James W., 13
Kean, Maria, 87
Keane, Patrick, 119
Kelly, John, 100
Kenefick, Teresa, 120
Kilkenny, 140
Kilmainham gaol, 137
Kilmore industrial school, 89, 101, 111, 146, 148
King's County gaol, 94
Kingsmill, Joseph, 25
Kirwan, Mrs, 42, 58–9, 70–1

labour *see* children's labour; employment; hard labour
lacemaking, 53, 109
larceny *see* stealing

laundry, 42, 53, 54, 65, 107–10
Lavelle, Catherine, 120
Lentaigne, John, 42, 49–51, 53, 57–8, 62, 69, 77, 85–9, 91–7, 100–1, 103, 106–13, 143–7, 152
Limerick, 121, 129
Limerick reformatory, 39, 53, 54, 69, 70, 74, 75, 108–9, 144, 149
literacy, 1, 96–7, 150
local authorities, 33, 47, 54, 124, 151
local gaols, 8–9, 31–2, 112–13, 116–17, 128–9, 135, 161–2
Lockwood, Mrs, 39, 70
London, 23, 30
Lynch, Rev. Francis J., 41, 48–9, 55, 56

McAvina, William, 102–3
MacCabe, F.X.F., 147
McGarry, Matthew, 101
MacHale, John, 26, 28
Mack, Peter, 123
McKenna, Patrick, 133
McKinney, William, 52
McMahon, Anthony, 122
Magdalene asylums, 35, 39, 53, 108
Maguire, John, 25–6, 27, 30, 33
Malone reformatory, 43–4, 51, 61, 63–4, 99, 104, 140–1, 144, 149, 160
manslaughter, 119, 120–1
marks system, 39, 41–2, 54, 61, 62
Mary of St Louis de Baligand, Mother, 53
Matthews, Mary, 111
Mayo county gaol, 113
Meagher, Thomas, 27–8
Meath, Reginald Brabazon, 12th earl, 151
medical officers, 16, 69, 102–3, 113
mental health, 101–2
Mettray reformatory, 19, 23, 30, 54, 56, 57, 75

military discipline, 30, 55–6
military service, 56, 154
Millbank prison, 102
Miller, Ian, 2
Mills, Margaret, 69, 74–5
Mitchel, John, 14
Monaghan, 42–3, 60–1, 66, 71–2, 74–5, 77, 105–8, 145
Mount St Bernard reformatory, 30
Mountjoy prison, 1, 9, 14, 30, 41, 100, 102–3, 136
murder, 120
Murray, Daniel, 38
Murray, Joseph, 120
Murray, Maria, 26–7
Murray, Patrick Joseph, 25, 28–9, 31, 38–40, 44–7, 49–56, 58–61, 63, 66–70, 72–7, 86, 158
Myles, Mary, 61

Naas, Richard Southwell Bourke, Lord, 32–3, 84
Nannetti, Joseph, 153
National Board of Education, 13
national schools, 26, 29, 66, 107
National Society for the Prevention of Cruelty to Children (NSPCC), 136, 150
needlework, 42, 52–3, 54, 65, 66, 75, 93, 107, 108, 110
Neilson Hancock, William, 82–3
Nenagh, 88, 99, 118–19
Nenagh gaol, 99
Netterville, Robert, 1
New Zealand, 109
Newgate prison, 30
Nolan, Patrick, 98
Norton, Charles Adderley, Lord, 146

Oblates order, 40, 49, 92, 103–4
O'Brien, Jane, 87
O'Brien, John, 121
O'Brien, William, 129

O'Callaghan, Mary, 66
O'Connell, Richard, 123
O'Conor Don, The, 83–4, 140, 143
O'Donel, C.J., 101, 111
O'Hagan, Thomas, 30, 31
orphanages, 26, 83
Osborough, Nial, 2
O'Shaughnessy, Robert J., 30
O'Sullivan, Eoin, 2
overcrowding, 12, 46, 50, 58, 61, 160

panopticon, 54
parents
  abscondees returned by, 58, 74
  behaviour in court, 3, 5, 101–2
  children encouraged into crime by, 11–12, 16, 24, 47, 74
  children neglected or badly treated by, 44, 47, 64, 73, 110–11
  financial contributions, 34–5, 47
  occupations of, 64
  petitions for release from, 96–7
  prosecution of children by, 111, 122
  responsibility, 24, 34–5
  visits to reformatories, 67
Parkhurst prison, 23
Parnell, Charles Stewart, 129
patronage societies, 103–4, 153–4
Peel, Robert, 45
penal servitude, 120, 139
petty sessions courts, 8, 34, 86–8, 99, 123, 130, 133
Philanthropic Reform Association (PRA), 134, 136, 139, 150, 151
Philanthropic Society, 23, 104
Philipstown reformatory, 88, 90, 92–5, 99–104, 123, 132, 143–4, 146–8
photography, 1, 4, 98
Plunkett O'Farrell, George, 147–8, 153

police, 12, 34, 70, 82, 86, 88, 98, 111, 119, 123, 129, 133, 142
Poor Law commissioners, 19, 20–1, 92
poverty, 4, 8–12, 22, 64, 80–2, 90–1, 119, 145, 150–1
Power, James, 120–1
Presbyterianism, 83–4
Prevention of Cruelty to Children Act, 150
prison registers, 4, 9, 118–23
prisons
  abuse, 137
  bridewells, 8, 135
  in Britain, 23, 102, 136–7
  chaplains, 15, 16, 18, 39, 113, 128, 135, 136
  children held in while awaiting trial, 128–9, 138
  closures, 135, 154
  construction, 9
  deaths, 9, 52
  discipline, 17, 54, 113–14
  education, 1, 13–14, 115–16
  food, 9, 12
  hard labour, 13, 16, 21, 61, 99, 119
  health, 9, 12, 13
  local gaols, 8–9, 31–2, 112–13, 128–9, 135, 161–2
  medical officers, 16, 69, 102–3, 113
  overcrowding, 12
  regulation and inspection, 113–15, 162
  separation of adult and child prisoners, 15–16, 115–17, 136
  visits, 136
  vocational training, 14, 136
Probation of First Offenders Act, 131–2
Probation of Offenders Act, 133

probation system, 131–3, 162
probationary industrial schools, 89, 101, 146, 148
proselytism, 25–8
prostitution, 24, 74, 81, 122
Protestantism, 26–9, 33–4, 39–41, 43–4, 46, 83–4, 104, 109, 148–9, 158, 159

Raftery, Mary, 2
ragged schools, 18–19, 25, 27
rape, 119
Rauhe Haus reformatory, 19
Reading gaol, 136–7
Redhill reformatory, 19, 104
reformatories
  Aberdare Commission enquiry, 5, 139, 140–7, 152, 160–1
  abuse, 56–7
  abscondings, 35, 58, 61, 71–2, 74–5, 94–5, 97–9, 109–10, 115–16, 122–3, 143, 160
  in Britain, 4, 18–19, 23–4, 30, 55, 58, 68, 104, 131, 139–40, 145, 158
  children's labour, 42, 47, 50–4, 61, 63, 65, 68, 75, 92–3, 104, 107–10, 160
  children's lives after discharge, 72–5, 99–105, 107–8, 109, 110–12, 151–3
  closures, 148–9, 154–5, 161
  daily life, 4, 63–72
  deaths, 93, 95
  discipline, 4, 30, 39, 41–2, 54–62, 69–70, 94–5, 97–9, 102–3, 105, 143–4, 160
  education, 63, 65–6, 68, 93, 96–7, 104, 107, 108
  establishment, 4, 23–4, 30–6, 39–46, 158–9
  in Europe, 4, 18, 19, 23, 29, 30–1, 56, 57
  food, 22, 55, 62, 63, 107
  funding, 4, 19, 23–4, 33–5, 43–4, 47–54, 75–7, 107–9, 140–1, 160
  health, 93, 95–6, 107, 110
  overcrowding, 46, 50, 58, 61, 160
  purpose-built facilities, 44, 49, 75, 104, 108–9
  release on licence from, 50, 97–8, 103–4, 140, 154
  and religion, 4, 25–9, 32–6, 38–46, 104, 158
  supervision of discharged children, 103–4, 107–8, 112, 153–4
  visits, 67
  vocational training, 52–3, 92, 104, 107, 108, 141
Reformatory Schools (Ireland) Act, 4, 34–5, 40, 58, 124, 158–9
Rehoboth Place reformatory, 43, 54, 61, 104, 118, 143
Reidy, Conor, 2
release on licence, 50, 97–8, 103–4, 140, 154
religion
  chaplains, 15, 16, 18, 39, 113, 128, 135, 136
  and education, 26–8, 38, 158
  proselytism, 25–8
  and reformatories, 4, 25–9, 32–6, 38–46, 104, 158
  religious education, 19
  and sentencing practices, 159
  see also Catholicism; Presbyterianism; Protestantism
reoffending, 74, 75, 99–101, 105, 108, 110, 112, 146, 152–3
restraints, 58, 69
Richmond bridewell, 12–14, 41, 113, 114–15, 128, 135
robbery, 20, 99; see also stealing
Robins, Joseph, 1
Rodenberg, Julius, 64
Roscommon, 123

Rosminian order, 44
Rothe, Eliza, 70
Rourke, Mary, 111
Royal Commission on the Administration of Prisons (1884–5), 128
Ruysselede reformatory, 30–1
Ryan, John, 47
Ryan Report, 2

St Louis order, 42–3
Salthill industrial school, 86–7
Sargent, Paul, 2, 29, 46, 55, 133
schoolmasters, 1, 13–14, 16, 93, 97, 115
Scully, Vincent, 25, 27
Seery, Margaret, 65
Select Committee on Criminal and Destitute Juveniles (1852–3), 18–23
Select Committee on Poor Relief (1861), 80–1
Senior, Edward, 20–1, 22
sewing *see* lacemaking; needlework; tailoring
shoemaking, 14, 61, 66, 68, 92, 110–11
Shore, Rev., 39, 43
Sisters of Charity, 29
Sisters of Mercy, 29, 42, 45
Sisters of Our Lady of Charity, 35, 39
Sligo gaol, 114
smallpox, 95
Smith, Mary, 105
Smithfield prison, 14
Smyth, Rev. Richard, 40–1, 48, 49, 56–7, 76
Society for Irish Church Missions (ICM), 26–7
Society of St Vincent de Paul, 30
solitary confinement, 62, 94, 102, 144
solitary working, 55

South Dublin Union, 57, 59, 81
Spark's Lake reformatory, 42–3, 60–1, 66, 71–2, 74–5, 77, 104–8, 141, 144–5, 149
Spike Island prison, 14, 15, 100, 102
Statistical and Social Inquiry Society, 100
stealing, 4, 11–12, 24, 55, 64–5, 87–8, 105, 111, 114, 118–19, 122, 131, 133, 143; *see also* burglary; robbery
Stevens, Patrick, 98
stone-breaking, 13
street trading, 151
Stretton-on-Dunsmore reformatory, 19, 23
suicides, 52, 93
Sullivan, John, 122–3
Summary Jurisdiction Act, 34
Summary Jurisdiction over Children Act, 129–30
summary trials, 17, 34, 117–18, 129–30
Summerly, John, 86
Swiney, Jacob, 149

tailoring, 14, 61, 68, 92
Taylor, Fanny, 59
Taylor, Mary, 109
theft *see* stealing
Tobin, Mary, 105
Toth, Stephen, 71
Townsend, Edmond Paul, 30
Tracey, William, 44, 64
Tralee, 119
transportation, 4, 8, 15, 16
treadmills, 13
Treasury funding, 23–4, 34, 47, 49, 54, 85, 108, 124
trespass, 8, 11, 122
Turner, Sydney, 25
typhoid, 95
Tyrrell, James, 40

Upton reformatory, 44, 50–2, 68, 73–4, 88, 100–1, 103–4, 117, 119, 144, 146, 149, 152

vagrancy, 9–11, 13, 22, 82–5, 117; *see also* begging; homelessness
Vagrancy Act, 8, 9, 12
van Verevenhaven, Emilie, 53
Vance, John, 84
Vincent, Howard, 131
visits, 67, 136
vocational training, 14, 52–3, 92, 104, 107, 108, 136, 141
voluntary contributions, 23–4, 47, 48–9, 53–4; *see also* fundraising

Wallace, Margaret, 8, 15
Walsh, Edward, 14
Walsh, John, 50
Webbe, William, 102
Whelan, James, 121
whipping *see* corporal punishment
Whipping of Offenders Act, 144
Wilde, Oscar, 136–7
Wines, E.C., 42, 57–8
Woodlock, Ellen, 42
workhouses, 4, 8, 9, 11, 19–21, 44, 48, 57, 59, 80–2, 87, 117, 122–3, 128

Young, Bernard, 52
Youthful Offenders Act, 132–3, 138